The Dharma
That Illuminates All Beings Impartially
Like the Light of the Sun and the Moon

by Kyabje Dorje Chang

KALU RINPOCHE

with a teaching by Lama Norlha

translated by Janet Gyatso

Edited by The Kagyu Thubten Choling
Translation Committee

THE DHARMA

That Illuminates All

Beings Like the Light

of the Sun

and the Moon

State University of New York Press

The eight auspicious symbols are
from *The Torch of Certainty* by Jamgon Kongtrul,
translated by Judith Hanson.
©1977 Judith Hanson and Shambhala Publications, Inc.
Reproduced by arrangement with Shambhala Publications, Inc.,
314 Dartmouth Street, Boston, MA 02116.

The photographs facing the Introduction, Chapter 6,
and Appendix I were taken by Sharon Mumby.
The cover photograph is by Felice Matare.

Published by
State University of New York Press, Albany

©1986, Kagyu Thubten Choling

For information, address State University of New York
Press, State University Plaza, Albany, N.Y., 12246

Library of Congress Cataloging in Publication Data

Karma-raṅ-byuṅ-kun-khyab-prin-las, Khenpo Kalu.
    The dharma that benefits all beings impartially
like the light of the sun and the moon.

    Includes index.
    1. Buddhism—Doctrines. I. Norlha. II. Gyatso,
Janet. III. Title.
BQ4165.K365   1986   294.3'42   86-5941
ISBN 0-88706-156-7
ISBN 0-88706-157-5 (pbk.)

10 9 8 7 6 5 4

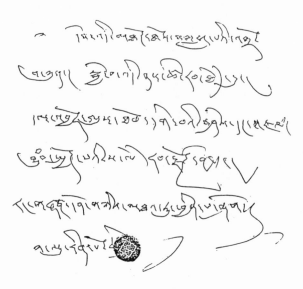

deb 'di mthong thos bklag pa'i 'gro ba kun
skye ba 'di nas tshe rab thams cad du
dal 'byor lus thob dge ba'i bshes dang mjal
byang chub spyod pa'i sa lam rab rdzogs nas
rang gzhan don gnyis mtha' ru phyin par shog.

ka lu rin po che

May all beings who see, hear, or read this book
In this life and all successive lives
Obtain the precious human body and meet with
        Friends of Virtue.
Having completely perfected the paths and stages
        of Bodhisattva conduct,
May they complete the Two Objectives: benefitting
        themselves and others.

Kalu Rinpoche

Table of Contents

Preface

Most of the teachings presented here were given orally by Kalu Rinpoche in 1982 at Kagyu Thubten Choling, his retreat center in upstate New York. They provide an authentic introduction to the foundations of Buddhism as taught in its three Vehicles—the Hinayana, Mahayana and Vajrayana—and offer groundings in Buddhist analysis, conduct, and practice for beginning and advanced students.

The compilation is thoroughgoing, and addresses an unusually wide audience: scholars will find here otherwise hard-to-find materials from the Karma and Shangba Kagyü traditions, practicioners will find fundamentally useful methods, and others will find a fascinating account of human and non-human affairs and conditions.

Kalu Rinpoche is one of the great meditation masters of the Buddhist tradition, whose teachings have been sought by all four schools of Buddhism in Tibet. The original extemporaneous translations of the teachings gathered here have been edited for the page in such a way as to preserve, at least partially, their oral character. The editors have also tried to preserve this quality in Lama Norlha's account of the Five Skandhas, which combines formal academic exposition with practical meditation instruction in a way that is characteristic of his lineage. (Lama Norlha, an accomplished meditation and retreat master, is Kalu Rinpoche's representative in the Eastern United States.)

Whenever a teaching is given in the Vajrayana tradition, it is the invariable custom for the teacher to begin by reminding the audience that the purpose of Buddhist learning and practice is to benefit all beings impartially, without exception. This is the idea that Kalu Rinpoche expresses in the title of his book, and this has been our purpose in bringing his teachings to a wider public. May all beings find happiness and be free from suffering.

Kagyu Thubten Choling
Wappingers Falls, New York,
1986

A Note

Tibetan terms are given in two ways: a pronouncing transcription which by and large tries to reflect the pronunciation of the author's region, and a strict transliteration (in square brackets) according to the Turrell Wylie system.

The Translation Committee of Kagyu Thubten Choling is responsible for editing Kalu Rinpoche's chapters, while Lama Norlha's teachings on the Five Skandhas were translated by Dr. Janet Gyatso. The Committee wishes to express its gratitude for many suggestions, emendations and clarifications received from a number of generous scholars and students.

Introduction: Kalu Rinpoche

Kalu Rinpoche was born in the district of Treshö Gang chi Rawa in the Hor region of Kham, Eastern Tibet, in 1905. This mountainous area, bordering on China, is known for the independent spirit of its people. His father, Karma Lekshe Drayang [ka rma legs bshad sgra dbyangs], the thirteenth Ratak Palzang Tulku, was noted for his skill in the practice of medicine, as well as for literary accomplishments and mastery of Vajrayana meditation practice. He and his wife, Drolkar Chung Chung [sgrol dkar chung chung], Rinpoche's mother, were students of Jamgon Kongtrul Lodrö Taye ['jam mgon kong sprul blo gros mtha' yas], Jamyang Chentse Wangpo ['jam dbyangs mkhyen brtse dbang po] and Mipham Rinpoche, all founders and leaders of the *ri may* [ris med] movement which revitalized the religious life of Tibet towards the end of the 19th Century by minimizing the importance of sectarian differences and emphasizing the common ground of the lineages and stressing the importance of meditation.

Both husband and wife were devoted to practice, and immediately after their marriage undertook a religious retreat. They saw little of each other during this period, but one night together each dreamed that they were visited by the great meditation teacher and scholar, Jamgon Kongtrul, who announced that he was coming to stay with them and asked to be given a room. Not long afterwards Drolkar Chung Chung discovered she was pregnant.

The dream had been auspicious; the pregnancy passed joyfully, without complications. Drolkar Chung Chung continued to work with her husband, and was gathering medicinal herbs with him one day when she realized the baby would soon be born. As they hurried back to their house, they saw the sky full of rainbows.

Such signs were interpreted in the neighboring countryside as portending the birth of a special incarnation. Conventionally, a *tulku* would have been taken to be raised in a monastery at the earliest possible age, but Karma Lekshe Drayang refused to follow this course. If the boy were not a high incarnation, he said, the training would be wasted; if he were, he would be quite capable of seeking the appropriate teachers and education for himself. That is just what he did.

"In his early years," the young man, "when he had awakened the excellent habits of virtue, and abandoned concerns for possessions and pleasures of this life, wandered at times in the wilderness of mountains and gorges, cliffs and crags. Spontaneously, uncontrived longing and resolution arose in him to nurture Dharma practice." Travelling freely in the mountains, Rinpoche would chant mantras, blessing the animals, fish or insects he might encounter.

At home, his education was supervised, rather sternly, by his father. After a preliminary training in grammar, writing and meditation, Rinpoche began his formal studies at Palpung [dpal spungs] monastery at the age of thirteen. At that time, the eleventh Tai Situ Rinpoche, Pema Wangcho Jalpo [pa dma dbang mchog rgyal po], gave him *getsül* [dge tshul] ordination, naming the young monk Karma Rangjung Kunchap [ka rma rang byung kun khyab]. The prefix "Karma" identifies Rinpoche as a practitioner of the Karma Kagyu tradition, and "Rangjung Kunchap" means "self-arisen, all-pervading."

At Palpung and elsewhere in Kham, Rinpoche studied the teachings of the sutras and tantras, receiving both instruction and empowerments from many of the great lamas. At the age of fifteen, during a *yarnay* [dbyar gnas], the traditional rainy-season retreat instituted by Buddha Shakyamuni, Rinpoche gave a profound and instructive discourse on the three vows before an assembly of a hundred monks and lay people.

At sixteen, Rinpoche entered Kunzang Dechen Ösal Ling, the retreat center (drup khang [sgrub khang]) founded by Jamgon Kongtrul Lodrö Taye, one of the two retreat facilities associated with Palpung monastery. Here he completed the traditional three-year retreat under the direction of the retreat master, his Root Lama (tsa way la ma [rtsa ba'i bla ma]) the Venerable Lama Norbu Tondrup [nor bu don sgrub], from whom he received the complete transmission of the Karma Kagyü and Shangba Kagyü traditions.

At the age of twenty-five, Rinpoche departed to do an extended solitary retreat in the desolate mountains of Kham, wandering without possessions, taking shelter wherever he could find it, seeking and needing no human company.

For twelve years he lived like this, perfecting his practice and offering everything to develop impartial love and compassion for all beings. "There is no higher siddhi than Compassion," his Root Lama had said. In this manner of life he would have been content to continue, had Situ Rinpoche not finally sent word that it was time for him to return to the world and teach.

Kalu Rinpoche returned to Palpung and assumed duties as director (drup pön [sgrub dpon]) of the three-year retreats. At this time Rangjung Rikpay Dorje, the late sixteenth Gyalwa Karmapa, recognized Rinpoche as the activity emanation (tin lay tül ['phrin làs sprul]) of Jamgon Kongtrul Lodrö Taye.* It was recalled that Jamgon Kongtrul had prophesied that his activity-incarnation would be a *ri may* master, dedicated to promoting practice and retreat.

In the 1940s he began visiting monasteries, traditional centers of many schools and lineages, all over Tibet, and on a visit to Lhasa gave teachings to the Regent of the young Dalai Lama.

In 1955, a few years before the full Chinese military occupation of Tibet, Rinpoche visited the Gyalwa Karmapa at Tsurphu, who asked him to leave Tibet in order to prepare the ground in India and Bhutan for the inevitable exile. Rinpoche first went to Bhutan, where he established two retreat centers and ordained three hun-

---

*There were at the same time four other incarnations of Jamgon Kongtrul, those of his body, speech, mind, and qualities. Of these the incarnation of mind, Jamgon Chentse Öser [mkhyen brtse 'od zer], was a resident tulku at Palpung and, along with Tai Situ Rinpoche, a root guru of the Gyalwa Karmapa. Jamgon Chentse Öser was also a teacher and friend to Kalu Rinpoche, as was Jamgon Pema Trimay [pa dma dri med], another of the five Jamgon Tulkus and a teacher at the Nyingma monastery of Shechen in Eastern Tibet.

dred monks. Proceeding to India, he made an extensive pilgrimage
to all the great Buddhist sites. In 1965 he established his own
monastery, Samdrup Tarjay Ling [bsam sgrub dar rgyas gling], at
Sonada near Darjeeling, where he now resides. A few years after
founding the monastery, Rinpoche established a three-year retreat
facility there, and has founded others elsewhere in India.

Since 1971 Kalu Rinpoche has travelled four times to Europe
and North America, establishing Dharma centers and facilities for
Westerners to undertake the traditional three-year retreat. At
Sonada in 1983 he gave to the four great heart-sons (tuk say [thugs
sras]—i.e., close disciples or successors) of the late Gyalwa Karmapa, as well as to thousands of tulkus, lamas, monks, nuns, and
lay people, the great cycle of empowerments called the "Rinchen
Ter Dzö" [rin chen gter mdzod], one of the "Dzö Chen Nampar
Nga" [mdzod chen rnam par nga] or "Five Great Treasuries" of
teachings and empowerments gathered by Jamgon Kongtrul Lodrö
Taye.

Kalu Rinpoche's recent activities, and particularly his four trips
to the West, are discussed in the first chapter of this book.

1

Kalu Rinpoche on Teaching in North America

I have been four times now to the North American continent. My first visit was in 1971; the Venerable Chogyam
Trungpa Rinpoche was already teaching here and the characteristic
style he had found it necessary to adopt was to present Buddhism
from the point of view of Americans. Instead of teaching in the
traditional manner, he found many skillful ways of presenting the
teachings in the light of worldly fields of knowledge, so that people
unacquainted with Buddhism could adapt their thinking to the
Buddhist view. In this way he was gradually able to introduce the
teachings to a large number of people.

This was a splendid undertaking, made possible by his own personal qualities, his superb command of English, and the fact that he
was to reside regularly in the United States. For my own part, I was
only staying here for about a year at most, that first time, so I felt
very strongly that if I were going to accomplish anything, I would
have to teach the Dharma in a traditional way, without combining it
with any other viewpoints.

To do this as clearly as possible, I gave teachings that I felt were
basic to the understanding and actual practice of Dharma. So I

taught extensively on the Four Thoughts that Turn the Mind — the four basic contemplations in Buddhist practice — and, in particular, on the concept of karma, the law of cause and effect that shapes our experience.

Before the introduction of the Buddhadharma to Tibet, the Land of Snows was a very barbaric place; there was little difference between its people and cannibal demons or primitive savages. Then a king arose among the Tibetan people whose name was Song-tsen Gampo [Srong btsan sgam po] and who is believed to have been an emanation of the Bodhisattva of Compassion, Chenrezi. Because of his miraculous powers, this king was able to bring the entire region we know as Tibet under his control, and from that political base he spread the Dharma throughout Central Asia. He was particularly devoted to meditation on Chenrezi, and under his influence that teaching spread very widely. As a result, Tibet became a sphere of activity for the Bodhisattva of Compassion, and Chenrezi became so embedded in the Tibetan consciousness that any child who could say the word "mother" could also recite the mantra OM MANI PADME HUNG*. Through this widespread meditation on Chenrezi, many people came to Realization.

From this beginning, the entire corpus of Buddhist teachings, both sutra and tantra traditions, with all the root texts and commentaries, was gradually brought from India to Tibet, and was translated and transmitted effectively and completely, without any element missing, to the Tibetan people.

In the great hope that this same sort of transmission will occur in the United States, Canada, Europe and all the countries of the West, I taught the Four Thoughts, the four contemplations that turn the mind from samsara towards practice. With this as a foundation, I taught extensively the Buddhist concept of Refuge and gave the Refuge vows. I also encouraged practice of Chenrezi meditation by giving the initiation (wang [dbang]) and instruction (tri ['khrid]) for it wherever I went. The results I felt to be very favorable.

The concept of Refuge and actually taking Refuge are fundamental to Buddhist practice; without this initial commitment, any further level of ordination or involvement is impossible. Refuge is the indispensable foundation for travelling the Buddhist path to

---

*Tibetans often pronounce this mantra: OM MANEE PAYMAY HOONG.

enlightenment. During the actual refuge ceremony I gave 'Refuge Names' to the participants, each beginning with "Karma." This is like a family or generic name, and indicates not only that these men and women had become Buddhists and had accepted the Three Jewels as sources of inspiration, but that they were connected, in particular, with the Karma Kagyü lineage. To the present day I have never changed my custom of giving this kind of Refuge name along with the vows of Refuge.

Because all meditational deities (*yidams*) are emanations of enlightenment, not one of them is without blessing—the power to aid and benefit beings. The form of Chenrezi, however, represents the quintessence and union of the love and compassion of all Buddhas and Bodhisattvas, of all enlightened beings. Meditation on Chenrezi can arouse that love and compassion in practitioners and thus can create a movement towards the realization of Emptiness and meditative absorption. That is why I chose this particular *yidam* to present to Western audiences.

The second journey I made to North America was in 1974. Because of the groundwork laid on my previous visit, I was able to present the Extraordinary Preliminary practices, the *Ngöndro* [sngon 'gro]. (These involve five practices each performed 100,000 times.) This stage of the teachings was emphasized during my second trip.

All the main schools of Tibetan Buddhism—Sakyapa, Gelugpa, Kagyüpa, and Nyingmapa—teach the Four Ordinary Foundations (the four thoughts that turn the mind towards Dharma practice) and the extraordinary preliminaries. I chose to teach the particular form of *Ngöndro* belonging to my own lineage, the Karma Kagyü; these practices are known as the preliminaries for the development of Mahāmudrā. In doing so, I encouraged people to focus on four aspects of meditation:

— To develop their devotion and sense of taking Refuge in the Three Jewels, and to develop bodhicitta—the enlightened or altruistic attitude of benefitting others which is based on love and compassion for all beings;

— To purify themselves of negative factors and obscurations through practicing the Dorje Sempa [rdo rje sems dpa'] meditation;

—To accumulate merit and deepen their awareness through the mandala offering; and

—To open themselves to the blessing of the lineage through Guru Yoga.

Another practice I introduced during this second visit was the practice of the Green Tara Meditation. This particular form of Tara is associated with her ability to protect and deliver us from fears and sufferings in this life and to aid us in our Dharma progress. With this threefold structure of formal practice—the preliminaries, the Chenrezi and the Green Tara Meditations—I established many centers that have continued to grow to the present day.

Although in each of the four schools of Tibetan Buddhism there are lineages leading to complete enlightenment, and although there is no difference at that ultimate level between the schools, I felt very strongly that it was important to maintain the identity of the Kagyü lineage. There were several reasons for this. First, the transmission of blessing is likely to be broken if the lineages are confused or if there is a sudden breakdown in their continuity. Secondly, I felt it important for people to understand exactly each transmission of the teaching they were practicing, so that they could receive the particular blessing associated with that lineage. To keep this Kagyü Mahāmudrā lineage very clear, then, I composed a prayer to allow an unending identification on the disciple's part with the actual lineage of the Mahāmudrā teachings.

During my third visit, in 1977 and 1978, I felt it was time to take one more step in presenting the teachings, and I decided to emphasize especially what in Tibetan we call *shi nay* [zhi gnas] and *lha tong* [lhag mthong], respectively tranquility meditation and the meditation that develops insight into the nature of the mind. I emphasized both ordinary techniques, common to all schools of Buddhism, and also some special instructions which are particular to my lineage. This was the main focus of my third visit.

Up to this point quite a lot of ground had been covered. There had been a presentation of the particular preliminary practices associated with the Mahāmudrā lineage, and of the teachings of the Chenrezi meditation, and of the techniques of *shi nay* and *lha tong*.

When His Holiness the sixteenth Karmapa arrived in India from the West in 1980, he landed at Siliguri airport before travelling by car to Rumtek in Sikkim; everyone from my monastery came down from Darjeeling to meet him. He spent the night in a hotel in Siliguri, and that evening said something along these lines to me: "If we add them all up, we now have some three hundred twenty Kagyü centers throughout the world. Every one of them needs guidance and support so that the people associated with them can come to a pure and sincere practice of Buddhadharma. Now, even though you're quite old, you're presently enjoying good health, so it's necessary for you to go to the West again, to visit these centers and give them all the help and guidance you can."

His Holiness then insisted that I perform the Kalacakra Empowerment in New York City in order to aid the general process of transmitting the teachings to the West. He was quite firm about this. He wouldn't accept any answer but yes and wanted me to return to New York as soon as possible for this purpose. So I agreed and came here as soon as I could.

That Empowerment has now been given, and through receiving it, people have made a good connection with the teachings, since the Kalacakra may be considered a summit of the Vajrayana tradition. I feel, therefore, that at least one good foundation has been established for the presentation of Mahāmudrā, the pinnacle of Kagyü meditation. But in order to present these Teachings properly, I need first to discuss the concept of emptiness, or *Śunyata*, and must first say something about the nature of consciousness. Without this I don't feel that actual Mahāmudrā teaching will be very effective or that people will be able to perceive its profundity or relate to it effectively. Nonetheless, certain foundations have been laid and I believe we can begin to think about the presentation of Mahāmudrā teachings. I sincerely hope that the benefits people have experienced so far will continue and help them benefit from further teachings that discuss the nature of mind.

In presenting teachings like these, I speak about anything and everything I can, as much as I can, in order to transmit what I understand about Dharma.

If we have a piece of white cloth and we want to dye it another color—red, yellow, green—we make a pot of dye and we dip the cloth in. Now if that dye is effective, if it takes, the cloth changes color so that when we pull the cloth out it is no longer a white cloth but a green cloth or a red cloth or a yellow cloth. If we pull it out and it's still white, we know something's gone wrong, the dye hasn't taken. I feel the same way about teaching: if I teach and my teaching influences people's minds, changing their lives and benefitting them, then I feel that it has taken, that it has been effective. If on the other hand I teach and people don't understand, or having understood don't do anything about it, if they listen and don't practice, then the dye has not taken.

2

The Four Noble Truths

The First Turning of the Wheel of Dharma

Two thousand five hundred years ago, after the Buddha achieved Enlightenment at Bodhgaya in India, he decided to present the teachings we now know as Buddhadharma to all sentient beings in order to liberate them. But he also understood that even if he did present these profound teachings, very little benefit would arise, since few would listen and accept what he said. In fact, seeing that people were unfit to receive the nectar-like teachings of the Dharma, the Buddha at first chose to avoid teaching altogether and went into the forest to rest and meditate alone. For three weeks he remained absorbed in the experience of Enlightenment and gave no teaching at all. But then two of the highest gods in the realm of samsara, Indra and Brahma, approached him; Indra presented him with a large white conch shell and Brahma presented a golden wheel with a thousand spokes. These gifts were symbols of the turning of the wheel of Dharma, and also signified a sincere request to present the teachings for the benefit of all beings. In response, the Buddha left the forest and at a place known as the Deer Park, in Sarnath, near Varanasi, India, he gave his first formal teaching. This teaching we now know as the teaching on the Four Noble Truths (pak pay denpa shi ['phag pa'i bden pa bzhi]).

Although the Buddha was completely aware of all the teachings that would ultimately be needed to discipline and lead beings to Enlightenment, and even though he was fully capable of presenting them, he also realized that the time had not yet come to introduce people to the profound concepts of the higher vehicles, the Mahayana and Vajrayana. He saw that serious misunderstandings would follow if he began by telling people that all phenomena were empty, that all experience was essentially empty, and that everything was really a projection of mind. Without proper preparation people might simply adopt a nihilistic approach and conclude that nothing was meaningful or made any difference. They might think that whatever they did had no real consequence, and that they therefore were free to do whatever they wished. Furthermore, if everything was just a projection of mind, there was nothing they could do to improve their situation—things simply had to work themselves out. All such misunderstandings, the Buddha saw, were likely to occur if people heard the profound teachings of the Buddhadharma without proper preparation.

Even today, many people develop such erroneous views when they hear Mahayana teachings, and the very profound transformative techniques of the Vajrayana tantras are equally open to misinterpretation. If these people hear, for example, that in the Vajrayana there is theoretically no need to suppress or alter emotional confusion, because simply seeing the nature of emotional conflict is sufficient for Liberation, they can easily misunderstand, and take this to mean that nothing has to be done about the emotions. Some people even think the Vajrayana teaches that lust and anger should be indulged when they arise in the mind. So, even though the Buddha was capable of providing all Mahayana and Vajrayana teachings, he recognized that beings had not been suitably prepared to accept them, and chose, in his first formal teaching, the basic and simple Hinayana approach.

Half of this teaching is devoted to our situation in the world, and half to the transcendence of samsara—the achievement of Nirvana (nya ngen lay day pa [mya ngan las 'das pa]). First, he examined thoroughly what we experience as the world, and discerned ignorance as its basic cause, and emotional confusion and suffering as the results. Then, after stating this first Truth of Suffering (du ngal ji denpa [sdug bsngal gyi bden pa]) and the second Truth of the Origin of Suffering (kun jung gi denpa [kun 'byung gi bden pa]), he examined the next two: Enlightenment itself, which, because it brings about the cessation of all suffering, is known as the Truth of Cessation (gok pay denpa ['gog pa'i bden pa]) and the Path we travel toward Enlightenment, the Truth of the Path (lam ji denpa [lam gyi bden pa]).

The First Two Noble Truths: Suffering and the Origin of Suffering

The first two of the Four Noble Truths, then, deal with the nature and cause of samsara. The Buddha describes the basic, world-producing cause as fundamental ignorance in the minds of all beings. This ignorance and its consequences can be analyzed as Twelve links of Dependent Origination (ten drel chu nyi [rten 'brel bcu gnyis]) that form the basis for a description of our experience of the world. The sequence of these links, or *nidanas*, in the cycle of our experience is (1) fundamental ignorance, which leads to (2) karmic formations. These become expressed in (3) dualistic consciousness, which in turn is translated into (4) a sense of identification, and the initial differentiation of consciousness into (5) the various sense fields. Through these sense fields there is (6) contact with the phenomenal world; from contact arises (7) sensation. Based upon sensation arises (8) craving for experience, followed by (9) grasping. On the basis of this, the mind harbors a sense of (10) becoming, a will to be, and this causes an actual physical incarnation. Once incarnate in a physical body, the mind experiences the various stages of human existence: (11) birth, and (12) the aging process and the stages of life that eventually lead to and end in death. At death the mind is immersed in basic ignorance again, and the cycle is complete.

It should be noted here that the Buddha did not describe this cycle of rebirth as something that he had created: he made no claim to be the originator of the universe. Nor did he accept the idea that any god had made the universe. The universe is a projection of mind.

In the Mahayana and Vajrayana teachings we find mind described as being in essence empty (ngo wo tong pa [ngo bo stong pa]), but nevertheless exhibiting natural clarity (rang-shin selwa [rang bzhin gsal ba]) and unimpeded manifestation (nam pa man ga pa [rnam pa ma 'gag pa]). This teaching, however, is found only in the Mahayana and Vajrayana. In the Hinayana teachings, the Buddha did not speak of it immediately, but rather introduced a more easily understood approach in which he simply stated that the mind is empty, and has no limiting or defining characteristics such as color, shape, size, or location. Thus, at the Hinayana level, mind was described as fundamentally empty, and ignorance as the failure to experience that emptiness. From this ignorance develops the whole cycle of events known as the universe, as samsara, the cycle of rebirth.

The First Four Nidanas

The structure or pattern of the Twelve *Nidanas* or links of Dependent Origination can be applied to any aspect of the universe, macrocosmic or microcosmic, or to the experiences of beings in the universe. This is a complex topic, but if we look at the situation of a single individual in the context of one lifetime we can perhaps understand the process more clearly. Let us take the example of a being who dies.

At the moment of death a separation occurs between the individual's physical body and mind, and the mind is plunged into a state in which there is no conscious mental activity. In other words, the mind simply dissolves back into its own fundamental state of unconsciousness, the first *nidana*, which we term ignorance (ma rik pa [ma rig pa]). This is the first link in the chain of Dependent Origination. After this there is a gradual stirring of mental activity. This is the second link, which is termed *du che* ['du byed], the formations now beginning to arise in the mind. These patterns of stirring consciousness find full expression in what we term *nam she* in Tibetan [rnam shes], discursive consciousness, the ability of mind to recognize something other than itself as an object — to decide, this is this, this is that, and so on. This level of dualistic discursive consciousness is the third link in the chain of Dependent Origination. Thus, from a fundamental state of ignorance there arises in the mind a gradual stirring of formations which finds full expression in discursive consciousness.

From this basic dualistic or discursive consciousness there arises the sense of self, of "I." At the same time, whatever forms are seen, whatever sounds are heard—in short, whatever phenomena are experienced—are perceived as some version of "other." In this way there occurs a definite split into self and other. At this point, although there is no physical basis for consciousness, there is nevertheless a sense of embodiment, of an identity coalescing. There is also the sense of naming things in the phenomenal world. So the fourth *nidana* is termed *ming zuk* [ming gzugs], which means "name and form."

All of this is just a mental experience for a mind in the second phase of the after-death experience, the *si pa* bardo [srid pa bar do], since it completely lacks anything tangible. We cannot see a being in this bardo. Moreover, the mind of this being is also completely imperceptible: no one else can see its ignorance, its stirring, its manifestation of discursive consciousness, or the experiences of subject/object labeling. This unique state in the *si pa* bardo, a completely internal experience imperceptible to others, is termed *ming shi pung po* [ming bzhi phung po] in Tibetan. This means "the *skandhas* (or aggregates) of the four names," and refers to the first four stages of the *si pa* bardo: its stage of ignorance, the stage of the stirring of conscious formations, the stage of fullblown discursive consciousness, and the stage of labeling the world in terms of subject and object.

All this is merely a projection of mind. There is not, for example, a thing called "ignorance" that we can take out and dissect and examine; we can say only that "ignorance" is a label we put on a particular phase of the *si pa* bardo experience, and that such a phase does occur. These four stages have no concrete or tangible qualities whatever.

Because the bardo consciousness has no physical basis, a being in the after-death state is not subject to the normal physical limitations. No mountains, walls, oceans, or forests present barriers to the consciousness in the bardo. Whatever arises in the mind is directly experienced, and wherever the mind decides to go, it goes. So, in a certain sense, the Four Names is a rather miraculous state—it cer-

tainly transcends the ordinary physical limitations and the properties of the world we're used to. However, it is an entirely automatic
or blind result of our previous actions or karma, and nothing that
occurs here is a conscious decision on the part of the being; we are
simply buffeted around by the force of karma.

During this period of the bardo, there is a certain kind of clairvoyance, very rudimentary and not really under conscious control,
but nevertheless an ability to perceive the thoughts of others. There
is also a certain new sense of the mind's power, although this power
is also not consciously or intelligently controlled. Furthermore, a
great variety of experiences — hallucinations — occur during the *si pa*
bardo. For a person with virtuous karmic tendencies these experiences can be very pleasant and comfortable. But for beings with
unvirtuous karmic tendencies the experiences can be terrifying.

This force we term karma is not a conscious process. An example of it is the growth of a child from infancy to adulthood. The
child does not have to sit down and decide: "Tomorrow I'm going to
grow this much. The next day I'm going to grow that much."
Without our doing anything about it and, indeed, without our being able to do anything about it, growth simply happens. In a completely unconscious way a force causes the organism to grow. In the
same way, the aging process simply happens unconsciously, without,
and even against, any intention on the part of the person concerned.
These are two examples of what we mean by the force of karma at
work in our experience.

During the first week or two of the *si pa* bardo — the first
third of it — the impressions that arise in the mind of the deceased
person are very largely related to his or her previous existence. If a
man dies, he will have the impression during this part of the *si pa*
bardo of being a man, with his own former personality and state of
existence; a woman will have the impression of still being a female
existence, and so forth. In each case there will be impressions
relating back to the previous life. This is why the consciousness of a
bardo being is said to experience returning to its former home and
being able to see in some way, but usually not to make contact with,
the people it left behind. There will be the experience of arriving at
the home and of announcing, "I'm here, I'm home again." But then
there will be a feeling of not being able to make contact with the

people still living there, and this can produce intense pain, frustration, and rage. Or the understanding that one has died may arise, and that trauma can produce immediate unconsciousness: the shock is too great to endure and the mind simply blanks out.

After the first week or two of the after-death experience, the impressions one has of a body and an environment begin to relate more and more to the future existence towards which one is being impelled by one's karma.

The actual length of the *si pa* bardo experience varies a great deal from person to person. In general terms, the longest period is held to be roughly forty-nine days. The Buddha referred to this particular period in many different scriptures as the length of time that the consciousness could be expected to remain in the *si pa* bardo before physical rebirth occurred. After existence in a physical form is established, the possibilities for change are more or less exhausted, for the time being, and this is why the Tibetan custom arose of employing any means possible to aid the dead person during this period of forty-nine days after death. The family might ask a Lama to perform rituals for the benefit of the dead person, because during that seven-week period there is always the possibility that the blessing of the Lama and the merit of the deceased will permit some beneficial change to take place. This is why we have a particular ceremony in which the teacher is presented with the name and an effigy of the deceased, and attempts through meditation to attract that person's consciousness (which still relates to its previous existence), and to influence it through bestowing empowerment, instruction, and prayer; in short, the teacher makes every effort to effect a favorable rebirth for the person.

The Fifth through Ninth Nidanas

The next *nidana*, or link, the fifth of the twelve, is termed *chem che* [skye mched], which can be translated as "sense-field." Altogether, there are held to be twelve sense-fields, one for each of the six senses and one for each of the objects of the six senses. (The mind is considered a sixth sense because in and of itself it produces thoughts, though not necessarily related to the sensory environment.) Thus, there is sight and the form which is seen; there is the ear, and the sound which is heard, and so forth, making a total of twelve sense fields. The Tibetan word *chem che* means to "originate" and to "spread," meaning that the origin of each of these senses is in the sense organ, and the spread is the field of perception in which that particular organ operates—form for sight, sound for hearing and so forth. Although a being in the *si pa* bardo has no physical organs for vision, hearing, and so on, there is, nevertheless, the mental impression that all the sense fields are complete. Consequently, the mind of such a being can see, hear, smell, taste, touch, and think just as we can now, even though these perceptions are all projections of mind with no physical basis.

The sixth *nidana* is termed *rek pa* [reg pa], which literally means "touch," or "contact," in just the same sense that the hand makes contact with an object it touches. In this case the word means that there is contact between the six sense subjects and the six objects—for example, between the faculty of seeing and form; in a certain sense, mind touches form with this faculty of sight, it touches sound with the faculty of hearing, and so forth. Even though this is a mental state without any physical basis, it is also accompanied by tactile sensation, a feeling of actually being able to touch and make contact with some kind of embodiment.

Formed upon this initial contact is the seventh *nidana*, which we term *tsor wa* [tshor ba], meaning sensation or feeling. To see is to make contact with the form through the eye; then follows a sense of the attractive or disagreeable nature of what we see, and some value judgment about the experience. Thus the initial experience doesn't remain a simple contact. Physical contact, for example, is accompanied by the sensation of roughness or smoothness, heat or cold, and so forth. In addition, some thought or value judgment arises: "That's beautiful, I like it," or "That's horrible, I don't like it." All such feelings, arising from the initial contact, belong to the seventh *nidana, tsor wa.*

The eighth *nidana* is termed *se pa* [sred pa], which means "craving." If one is very hungry and sees delicous food, a craving develops for that food; likewise, in the consciousness of a being in the *si pa* bardo, once there is contact between the sense fields and their objects, there come to be feelings and sensations that lead to a further clinging to and craving for that kind of experience. This leads to the further state which we term *len pa* [len pa], the ninth *nidana*.

Len pa literally means "to take," and the image traditionally used is of someone picking fruit, actually taking fruit in the hand. Among the twelve *nidanas*, the stage of *len pa*, or grasping, is the one in which the will to take physical rebirth impels the mind toward incarnation. For a being about to be reborn as a human, this results in a perception of the future mother and father engaged in sexual intercourse. A tremendous attachment, a blind will to incarnate, draws the mind of the *si pa* bardo being towards the couple in union.

Becoming, The Tenth Nidana

The process of attraction to physical rebirth finds its completion, for a human being, when conception takes place in the mother's womb. This is the tenth *nidana, si pa* [srid pa] which means "becoming" or "existence." At this point there is a physical basis — union of the sperm from the father and the egg from the mother — and, as a third component, the entrance of consciousness. Thereafter, according to the teachings of the Buddha, we are speaking of a human individual. A monk or nun, for instance, vows not "to take the life of a human or a conceived entity that will develop into a human being." To take the life of even a fetus in the womb is to take the life of a human being. Conception represents the final outcome of the urge possessing the disembodied consciousness of the being in the *si pa* bardo to inhabit a particular realm. Once conception has taken place, the being has entered the human realm and will, in due course, be born, raised, and fully accepted as a human being among humans.

So when we have a blending of the two physical elements, the sperm and egg, and the one immaterial element, the consciousness of the being in the after-death state, a human individual is conceived. The consciousness has taken rebirth and is in a physical realm again. One might ask, "How does this come about, this blending of the material and the immaterial?" The point is that mind is fundamentally empty: mind itself is immaterial and has no solidity or corporeality. But because of fundamental ignorance, there is an inability to experience that immateriality, and a tendency to conceive of it in material terms such as "some thing" or "I," "me," and "mine." This mental tendency to solidify finds its fullest expression in physical rebirth—the conjunction of consciousness and the physical element brought about by fundamental ignorance.

Within the teachings of Buddha, the subsequent stages of fetal development are described in detail. During the first week or two an amorphous mass of cells (described in the traditional texts as being something like a small white blob of yogurt) grows slowly larger in the uterus. During the next stage the various parts of the body begin to differentiate, and the fetus, which now consists of two cellular masses connected by a narrow filament, is said to resemble an ant. Appendages begin to grow, organ systems develop and eventually, at the full term of the pregnancy, we have a fully developed human baby in whom all the complex processes of differentiation are complete.

There are definite experiences during the period of fetal development, a period of relentless growth during which the five bodily appendages (two arms, two legs and the head) emerge from the torso, and the five sensory organs and various organ systems are formed. In general, these are experiences of great suffering, and suffering, indeed, characterizes the entire period of gestation. Because growth within the mother's womb continues from conception to birth, and because during this period the embryo generally becomes a complete human individual able to survive outside the womb, the whole period of gestation belongs to the *nidana* of becoming. The *Sutra of Entering the Womb* (ngal juk pay do [mngal 'jug pa'i mdo]), which is basically a study in embryology, describes the whole process in considerable detail.

The Eleventh and Twelfth Nidanas

Towards the end of pregnancy the baby begins to become dimly aware of the confined, cramped conditions within its mother's womb, and directly before birth experiences a sense of oppression and claustrophobia. The karmic process of human birth entails a force in the mother's body which turns the child's head downwards in preparation for birth, and then labor contractions that force the child into the world. This brings us to the next *nidana*, the eleventh, that of actual physical birth, which is termed *che wa* in Tibetan [skye ba].

The final link in the chain of Dependent Origination is aging and death, *ga shi* [rga shi]. Aging begins at the moment of birth and continues up to the moment of death, regardless of the age at which one dies. Attendant on this relentless aging process are all the sickness, suffering, sorrow, and pain that a human being experiences.

The final *nidana* is this aging and death. The moment of death is followed by the separation of mind and body, and the arising of the fundamental state of unconsciousness — ignorance. So arriving again at the first *nidana*, this one lifetime has brought us full cycle. Following the state of unconsciousness, the cycle of twelve links continues with the stirring of the mind, the reawakening of discursive consciousness, and so on. This is one aspect of samsara, which literally means a cycle or wheel: it makes a complete cycle from lifetime to lifetime.

The Five Skandhas and The Three Aspects of Suffering

Having taken physical existence, we have a body composed of flesh and blood, and at a more fundamental level, of atoms. Through this vehicle we experience the world. Whereas in the *si pa* bardo state we referred to the *skandhas* of the Four Names as being purely a mental experience, here we have to add a fifth element of physical existence, which we term the *skandha* of form. In our present human condition there are five *skandhas*: the physical existence plus the four purely mental states of sensation, perception, mental formations, and full discursive consciousness which is able to decide — this is a sound, this is a form — and to arrive at value judgments — this is good, this is bad, and so on.

The word *skandha* literally means "a heap" or "pile," and one understanding of the term is that as long as we have physical existence, we not only have these five aggregates, but also a heap of trouble. On the basis of our physical existence all kinds of suffering — sickness, pain, aging, death, happiness followed by unhappiness — are possible. This fundamental potential, intrinsic to all compound things, is *chap pa du che chi du ngal* [khyab pa 'du byed kyi sdug bsngal], meaning "the Pervasive Suffering of Composite

Things." It is the most subtle kind of suffering because it exists simply in the fact of being alive. It may not be experienced directly as suffering, or be seen as something tangible or threatening, but it is nonetheless inseparable from the five *skandhas* in physical rebirth.

In traditional texts it is said that the difference between a noble (pak pa ['phags pa]) individual and an ordinary person is that the first perceives and the second does not perceive this subtle aspect of suffering. To illustrate this the following example is used. If you place a hair on the palm of your hand, you have no sensation of it. If, however, the hair is in your eye, it hurts and you are aware of it very promptly. An ordinary person, who has no sensation of the fundamental aspect of suffering, is like the palm of the hand in response to the hair; the noble person is like the eye—very much aware.

In addition to the Suffering of Composite Things, there is the Suffering of Change (jur way du ngal ['gyur ba'i sdug bsngal]. When a person in perfectly good health suddenly takes a turn for the worse, that change—that loss of something good—is the aspect of suffering called the suffering of change.

When we actually experience pain, suffering, and frustration, or one pain laid upon another, such as death following severe illness, then we speak of a third kind of suffering: actual pain, or, the Suffering of Suffering (du ngal ji du ngal [sdug bsngal gyi sdug bsngal]).

This, then, is a general account of the Buddha's teaching of the first two Noble Truths, the truth of the causes of suffering and the truth of the suffering we actually experience.

The first Noble Truth is termed the Truth of Suffering, and the second the Truth of the Origin [of Suffering]. The origin meant here is the ignorance that gives rise to the Twelve Links of Dependent Origination. The consequence of this cycle is suffering, and a traditional illustration of the samsaric process is a tree whose root represents ignorance and whose fruit is suffering.

The Suffering of the Different Realms

In the Buddhist tradition another way of looking at the universe is in terms of the three realms (kam sum [khams gsum]):

The Realm of Desire (dö pa'i kham ['dod pa'i khams]), the Realm of Form (zuk pay kam [gzugs pa'i khams]), and the Formless Realm (zu me chi kam [gzugs med kyi khams]). The Realm of Desire encompasses everything from the lowest hell up through the desire gods' realms. The six kinds of beings in the Realm of Desire are hell-beings, hungry ghosts, animals, humans, *asuras* and gods. Beyond it lie the seventeen levels of gods in the Realm of Form, and beyond that are the four levels of gods in the Formless Realm. But whatever the realm, and however subtle or gross the level of experience, it is included in the cycle of samsara, where no individual being is in any way separate from the three kinds of suffering, where no being finds a complete solution to any one of them.

The fact is that suffering is the fundamental, central experience of all life, in whichever realm of samsara it occurs. In the hell realms, for instance, beings experience intense heat and cold. In the hungry ghost realm, suffering is due to hunger, thirst, and affliction by the elements. In the animal realm stupidity and ignorance lead to blind, instinctive behavior and to the preying of one species upon another.

The situation and sufferings of beings in these three lower realms are mostly invisible to us. There are descriptions of them in the teachings of the Buddha, but we have no personal, direct evidence of them, except for what we can observe in a small part of the animal realm. If we examine animals in the ocean, or domesticated or wild animals, we can see the kinds of body these creatures inhabit and the kind of mentality they have. In this way we can gain a little understanding of what this lower realm of existence is like, and what kinds of suffering the beings in it may experience.

The Buddha once said, if we were really aware of suffering, if we weren't so ignorant, if we even understood the pain and suffering a fetus experiences in its mother's womb, then we would work hard in this lifetime to become enlightened and never experience such suffering again.

For example, if we remembered the pains of fetal development, we would remember that during the development of the different orifices and sensory organs, the pain is as though someone were sticking a finger into a open wound, probing it, and ripping it open. And we would remember that when the various appendages, the arms, legs, head and so forth, are developing, the pain is as though a very strong person were pulling our arms out of their sockets while someone else was beating them with a club. The development of the different organ systems—nerves, bones, muscles, digestive tract and so on—entailed similar pains, which would also be remembered.

Moreover, the mind of the fetus is very sensitive to the mother's physical condition. If the mother eats food which is very cold, the child feels as though it's being thrown naked onto ice. If the mother drinks or eats something extremely hot, the child feels as though it's being boiled or scalded. If the mother does not eat, the child feels as though it's suspended in space; if the mother eats too much, the impression is of being crushed by a mountain. If the mother engages in sexual intercourse, the child feels as though it's being beaten with thorns. If the mother runs or jumps or engages in any violent physical exercise, the child feels as though it's being thrown over a cliff, and bouncing down a mountainside. In addition to all this, there is the suffering of simply being in the womb: of being in a dark, cramped, oppressive space where there is also a sense of uncleanness, and a disagreeable smell arising from waste fluids.

The actual process of birth is extremely painful. In Tibet we have a certain device, a metal disc with a small hole in it, through which a large thread can be drawn to make it smaller and tighter. When a baby is compressed in the narrow space of the vagina and thrust into the world, it feels as though it were being drawn through just such a device. And once the baby has been born, it is extremely sensitive to the touch of anything in the outer world; it feels, as it comes into the world, like a small bird being attacked by wolves or hawks—an immediate, overwhelming experience of being handled, grabbed, and spun around in various ways. When the child is washed, it feels as though it were being flayed; and when it's laid down, however soft the cover that it's put on, it feels as though it were being stretched on a bed of thorns. Children invariably cry when they are born, a sign of suffering and distress; if the birth process were not painful, one would expect babies to be born smiling and laughing.

We have all experienced the various sufferings of the rebirth process described by the Buddha, but we don't remember. Most of us, though, and more especially doctors and people involved in medicine, are aware of the suffering of growing up and being alive in the world. We've experienced illness and various physical and mental problems, and we know that these are always followed by the pain and suffering of death. This is where we are sitting now: in the middle of all this suffering.

Within the context of human existence, however, there is a great range of individual experience. Some people experience great pain, suffering and hardship in life, while others live fairly comfortably, without much pain or distress. For example, the Third Karmapa, Rangjung Dorje, once said that his experience in his mother's womb had been very pleasant: he had felt like a god in one of the high desire realms, enjoying a most pleasant existence throughout the whole term of pregnancy. As for the Buddha himself, his power and realization were so strong that even in the womb of his mother, Queen Mayadevi, he was able to benefit many creatures through a certain kind of transmission of the Dharma.

Although in general we can say that suffering and pain attend all experiences, our own karma must always be taken into account. For those with especially virtuous karma, there will be a preponderance of happiness in any experience, and a lessening of suffering. Such circumstances are the results of the individual aspects of karma, as distinct from the common karma of human existence.

The realm of existence above ours in samsara, that of the *asuras*, approximates, in terms of splendour, wealth and enjoyment, the state of the gods. There is, however, such a strong element of envy in the minds of these *asuras* that they live in continual strife, always fighting and quarreling with each other and with the gods in an effort to rob them of their wealth. Strife and quarrel are the dominant characteristics of this realm of existence and attendant on them are constant suffering and pain.

The last of the six realms in the Realm of Desire is that of the gods. From a relative point of view this is the superior realm of existence, since it is marked by the greatest degree of happiness and contentment, and by a level of prosperity and sensual enjoyment we cannot begin to imagine. The most intense feeling of contentment and happiness a human can experience probably amounts to less than one percent of the total physical and mental bliss a god enjoys.

Nonetheless, the relative state of ease and comfort in the god realm is impermanent, and when the causal factor—the merit that has led to rebirth there—is exhausted, the gods fall to a lower state of existence. This fall is forecast by certain premonitions that begin seven days before the god will die and pass to a lower state. At first, the gods hear a voice speaking of impending death; then they begin to resemble a withering flower: the garlands of flowers they wear begin to decay and lose their fine scent; the body for the first time begins to sweat and smells disagreeable. Their companions, the gods and goddesses who shared the pleasures of the god realm with them, are utterly repelled by these signs of dying and flee, offering no more help or encouragement than the rain of flowers that they scatter behind them, and a sincere prayer that their future rebirth be used skillfully to regain the godly state and join them again. Beyond that, they simply abandon dying gods, leaving them to spend their last week alone, contemplating, with the limited prescience that gods have, their future state of rebirth. The dying gods feel great distress because that state will inevitably be a lower one. Moreover, this seven day period corresponds to seven hundred of our years, so the gods experience this suffering of change for a very long time.

For these reasons the Buddha, after examining the various realms, said that no place in the cycle of rebirth is free from sorrow: suffering is the central and fundamental experience of unenlightened existence.

The Importance of Studying the First Two Noble Truths

These, then, are the ideas the Buddha presented as the first two of the Four Noble Truths: the truth of the suffering we experience in the cycle of rebirth and its origin. The Buddha taught these subjects extensively and in great detail, and it is important for us to understand them in order to recognize the limitations of our present situation. We have to understand our circumstances and know that, given the nature of cause and effect, or karmic relationship, we can look forward to nothing but suffering. We have to realize that we are enmeshed in the various factors of cause and effect, which lead first to one state of suffering and on that basis to another, and so on. When we have seen the inherent limitations of this situation, we can begin to consider getting out of it. We can begin to look for the possibility of transcending samsaric existence and all its attendant sufferings, limitations, and frustrations.

If we have not examined these questions, our basic approach to existence will be naive. As long as we are happy and things are going well we think, "Oh, everything's fine. What's all this talk about suffering? Samsara's a nice place to be." From this attitude comes a general tendency to let things slide. But as soon as something untoward happens, the minute there is any kind of pain, or suffering, or trouble, we become completely unnerved. We think, "Oh, I'm dying. Oh, I'm sick. Oh, things are falling apart. Everything's going wrong." We may then make some ineffective and rudimentary attempts to remedy the situation, but we have no real recourse to anything that will allow us to transcend our suffering.

We are caught in samsara. As long as things go well, we ignore the situation; when they go badly, we are helpless to deal with them. But once we have understood the situation, we will begin to look for a way of dealing with the suffering and frustration we inevitably meet. The techniques and methods of the Buddhadharma provide the means for this positive development.

Ultimately speaking, the causes of samsara are produced by the mind, and mind is what experiences the consequences. Nothing other than mind makes the universe, and nothing other than mind experiences it. Yet, still ultimately speaking, mind is fundamentally empty, no 'thing' in and of itself. To understand that the mind producing and experiencing samsara is nothing real in itself can actually be a source of great relief. If the mind is not fundamentally real, neither are the situations it experiences. By finding the empty nature of mind and letting it rest there, we can find much relief and relaxation amidst the turmoil, confusion, and suffering that constitute the world.

Moreover, when there is a complete understanding and experience of the mind's Emptiness, we transcend causality: being beyond the cause and effect of karmic tendencies, we are a Buddha. But until this happens, simply thinking "It's all empty" is not going to do any good; we are still entirely subject to the unfailing process of karma.

Therefore, we need to understand not only the concept of the ultimate Emptiness of all experience, but also the conventional validity of karmic cause and effect. With this kind of approach, we can achieve Enlightenment. But if we fall into either extreme — either naively assuming the ultimate reality of everything (the error of the eternalists) or else denying everything (the error of the nihilists) — then we cannot achieve Enlightenment.

The Third and Fourth Noble Truths: The Truth of Cessation and The Truth of The Path

After the Buddha had described the Truths of Suffering and the Origin of Suffering, he went on to examine the other side: the factors of cause and result in the context of Nirvana. The cause here is the Fourth Noble Truth, known as the Truth of the Path. The result is the achievement of Enlightenment, and in the context of the Four Noble Truths this is called the Truth of Cessation, the Third Noble Truth. Enlightenment here is seen from the Hinayana viewpoint as the cessation of emotions that confuse and trouble the mind, and the cessation of the sufferings they cause.

The Beginning of the Path

Just as the first two Noble Truths describe samsara as arising from ignorance, from unknowing, so it follows that the enlightened experience arises from awareness (rik pa [rig pa]) instead of ignorance (ma rik pa [ma rig pa]). But such awareness is not easily experienced; we have to work towards it, and this is what constitutes Dharma practice. We adopt a virtuous and skillful way of life, avoiding actions harmful to ourselves and others, and engaging in actions that are helpful and positive. Then, motivated by the inclination to establish a connection with the Three Jewels — the Buddha, the Dharma (his teaching), and the Sangha (the community of his followers), we take Refuge, and continue to take Refuge, motivated by faith, devotion, and our ongoing experience of the Path. All these aspects of Dharma practice contribute to our experience of that awareness from which Enlightenment develops. The Seed of Enlightenment, this potential for Buddhahood, which we term *Tathagatagarbha*, is latent in every one of us, though in our present circumstances we cannot perceive it directly.

A rough analogy of our situation can be found in the process of sleep. When we go to sleep there is an initial period of complete unconsciousness, a very deep sleep in which there is no dreaming, no conscious activity at all. This state corresponds to the causal factor of fundamental ignorance. During the night, however, there is from time to time a certain reawakening of conscious activity, which produces the many kinds of illusion we call dreams. These can sometimes be very frightening, nightmarish experiences, which correspond to the suffering in samsara produced by ignorance. In the dream state, as in the waking experience of samsara, there is mental activity, which arises out of unawareness. In the morning, before we actually wake up, the body begins to stir, and consciousness starts to approach the waking state. For the purpose of our analogy, we can say this period corresponds to the arising of such virtuous tendencies in the mind as faith, compassion, energy, and exertion in Dharma practice. Then follows the actual awakening, when we stretch in bed, get up, begin to move around, and start our activities for the day. In our analogy, this corresponds to achieving Enlightenment — we have completely awakened. We are not just in the dream state, which is our present condition, and not just half awake in Dharma practice, which is instilling and developing these good qualities in us; instead, we are totally awake, able to get up and be effective.

Part of the fundamental process of turning our minds away from samsara and towards Enlightenment is understanding samsara for what it is. Understanding suffering, and recognizing the limitations of our present situation, we begin to seek a way out. This initial turning of the mind is the foundation of the Path in its aspect as a causal factor leading to Enlightenment. Our ability to follow the Path by actually undertaking Dharma practice has a twofold basis. First, because we have fostered virtuous tendencies and rejected unwholesome ones, we have achieved the basic state of a human being. Second, because of the efficacy and compassion of the Three Jewels, we have established a connection with the Dharma which is bearing fruit in this life: we are not only human beings, but humans who are in contact with the teachings of Dharma, and have developed some certainty or conviction in them that leads to practice. Our actual practice — taking Refuge in the Three Jewels, continuing to take

Refuge, developing Bodhicitta (our concern for the Liberation of each and every living being), developing different meditation techniques—constitutes the real pith or essence of the cause leading us towards the goal of Enlightenment.

Aspects of the Path

There are various aspects of the Path. For instance, we can look at the different levels of ordination starting with the vows of Refuge, then the vows of a layperson, a novice monk or nun, a fully ordained monk or nun, the Bodhisattva vows, and so on. Another aspect of the Path is *ngöndro* practice: the 100,000 recitations of the Refuge prayer accompanied by physical acts of prostration, the 100,000 recitations of the purification mantra of Vajrasattva, the 100,000 mandala offerings and the recitation of 100,000 prayers in the Guru-Yoga meditation. Both aspects—the levels of ordination and the graduations of *Ngöndro* practice—belong to what we term the Path of Accumulation (tsok lam [tshogs lam]), because this first stage of the Complete Path to Enlightenment is the gathering of what we need for the journey.

Yet practice aimed only at purifying our obscurations and developing merit is unstable because its benefits can be lost. Meditation practice provides the stabilizing factor by producing a benefit that will not be lost, but continues as a stable element of our experience. In particular, the practice of *shi nay* is important because whatever merit we accumulate, whatever virtuous tendencies we reinforce, all gain a degree of stability when the mind has been calmed. Moreover, whatever sort of meditation we attempt to develop is given a firm foundation by this initial phase of *shi nay* meditation. Therefore, when this stabilizing element has entered the picture, we speak of a superior degree of the Path of Accumulation.

There are various ways of examining the Complete Path. For example, we can speak of the Five Paths constituting its different levels: the Path of Accumulation, the Path of Application, the Path of Seeing, the Path of Meditation, and the Path of No More Learning, or Buddhahood. At a more extensive and detailed level are the Thirty-seven Elements which contribute to complete Enlightenment. All of these are different ways of examining the same phenomenon—all detail different aspects of Enlightenment.

Among the Thirty-seven Elements conducive to Enlightenment are four essential recollections, four proper attitudes towards what one should renounce and what one should accept, four bases for the development of supernormal power, five faculties, and five strengths which are developed in one's Dharma practice. All these elements pertain to the first two Paths, those of Accumulation and Application; they do not include the first level of Bodhisattva Realization, which corresponds to the Path of Seeing, the third of the Five Paths.

At present, when we talk about mind being empty, clear and unimpeded, we are simply expressing an intellectual concept. But as your Dharma practice progresses and develops, there comes a point where you actually have a direct experience of the mind as empty, clear and unimpeded. When this direct experience is stable, we refer to it as the first level of Bodhisattva realization. In Tibetan this is termed *rap tu ga wa* [rab tu dga' ba], meaning "complete joy." At this point you enter the Path of Seeing, because now, instead of seeing things in the ordinary sense, you actually see the nature of mind, and experience it directly. This moment of insight, therefore, lends its name to the Path at this particular stage.

The first level of Bodhisattva realization is termed a state of utter joy because the nature of mind, which is now experienced directly, is supremely blissful, supremely illuminating and, in the sense of not being anything ultimately real in and of itself, supremely empty. Although empty, the experience is one of complete bliss. The term used for this state is *de wa chen po* [bde ba chen po], "supreme bliss"—"supreme" because there is nothing in our ordinary experience we can compare it to. So, accordingly, direct experience of the nature of mind in its intrinsic purity is known as the state of complete joy.

At this stage of realization since you are no longer concerned with conceptual thought but with direct experience, you have greater freedom of mind. At the first level of Bodhisattva realization there is a freedom from the limitations of clinging to a self (dan dzin [bdag 'dzin]). This is why we can speak of the one hundred emanations a first level Bodhisattva can manifest in a single instant, or of the ability to recall a hundred previous existences, or to foresee a hundred future ones. These abilities belong to a partial, not a complete, freedom of the mind from the limits of ignorance, and we traditionally refer to the twelve aspects of this freedom as the Twelve Hundreds.

Moreover, a first level Bodhisattva has transcended the karmic process, and is no longer completely subject to its obscuring limitations. Awareness has replaced ignorance. Since fundamental discursive consciousness, *kun shi nam she* [kun gzhi rnam shes], is based on that ignorance, it too no longer obtains. *Kun shi nam she* functions as a kind of store-house for the karmic process, which is reinforced (1) by the obscuration of the emotional afflictions (nyön mong pay dri pa [nyön mongs pa'i sgrib pa]) that develop from dualistic clinging, and (2) by the physical, verbal and mental activities (lay chi dri pa [las kyi sgrib pa]) based on that obscuration. Without fundamental ignorance, the karmic process has no basis. Thus a first-level Bodhisattva transcends the obscuring limitation of karma.

In Tibet we use a lunar calendar. On the third day of any month the moon is just a thin sliver, which gradually increases until on the fifteenth day it attains complete fullness. This gradual waxing of the moon provides an image for the different levels of Bodhisattva realization. The first glimmering of awareness is like the thin sliver of the moon. It's there, but not fully developed. Where development takes place is in the continued deepening and extending of awareness, and in the increasing freedom of mind experienced at the ten different levels of Bodhisattva realization.

In the context of the increasing freedom of mind, the qualities known on the first level as the Twelve Hundreds are increased tenfold on the second level. So there we speak of the Twelve Thousands, of the ability to manifest a thousand emanations in a single instant, to recall a thousand previous existences, to foretell a thousand future existences, and so forth. This increase in depth and scope of awareness continues as we progress through the different stages of Bodhisattva Realization.

The waxing moon of the eleventh day, when the moon is not quite full but is rapidly approaching fullness, corresponds to the seventh level of Bodhisattva Realization. Here the increase in positive tendencies and the deepening of awareness accompany a diminishing of the negative aspects of one's being. In particular, emotional afflictions have been mostly eliminated at the seventh Bodhisattva stage.

At the eighth and ninth levels of Bodhisattva realization habitual dualistic clinging (bak chak chi dri pa [bag chags kyi sgrib pa]), which is the next most subtle level of obscuration, is gradually eliminated.

At the tenth Bodhisattva level, fundamental ignorance, the final level of obscuration (she jay dri pa [shes bya'i sgrib pa]), is almost completely removed, and the mind is almost completely without limitation. An enormous capability to express the positive qualities of mind arises. At this point we speak not of a hundred or a thousand emanations, but of one hundred thousand million emanations, previous lifetimes, future lifetimes, and so forth.

These ten levels of Bodhisattva Realization constitute the third and fourth Paths, the Path of Seeing and the Path of Meditation. Within this framework further levels are distinguished—the inferior, medium and superior levels of the Path of Seeing, and the inferior, medium and superior levels of the Path of Meditation—but in sum they coincide with the ten levels of Realization. Among the Thirty-seven Elements conducive to Enlightenment, the seven Branches of Enlightenment—mindfulness, investigation of dharmas (phenomena), diligence, joy, purification, samadhi, and equanimity—and the Noble Eightfold Path are experienced at these levels.

On the tenth level of Bodhisattva Realization, the final step to complete Enlightenment is accomplished by the particular state of meditation known as the Vajra-like samadhi (dor je ta bü ting nge dzin [rdo rje lta bu'i ting nge 'dzin]), where "vajra" has the sense of something invincible, something that can cut through anything else. And what is being cut through here are the final and most subtle traces of ignorance about the ultimate nature of reality. When this finest veil has been rent asunder by Vajra-like samadhi, we are completely enlightened. We have reached full and complete Buddhahood, sometimes called the eleventh Bodhisattva stage.

Our present circumstances are like those of someone who has been bound in chains and locked in a dark prison cell. The cell is samsara, and we are bound up and confined in it by our own ignorance. On the Paths of Accumulation and Application, up to but not including the first level of Bodhisattva Realization, there is a growing sense of freedom, just as if a person in prison were to have these bonds and manacles removed and, though still imprisoned, were free to move about the cell. The experience of first level Bodhisattva Realization, the Path of Seeing, resembles the opening of the prison door, after which we can walk out and go anywhere.

In this analogy, the prison represents the confining nature of samsara. The manacles and chains represent the limitations imposed by our own ego-clinging; regardless of which realm of samsaric existence we experience — regardless of where in the prison we may be — we are still chained by the impression of being a self, by the conviction that this ego ultimately exists. With the experience of the first and subsequent Bodhisattva levels we are freed from the shackles and then freed from the prison.

The Three Kayas

Buddhahood, complete Enlightenment, is described in terms of the Three Kayas (three bodies) (ku sum [sku gsum]). These three aspects of complete Enlightenment are known as the Dharmakaya, Sambhogakaya and Nirmanakaya. The three are related to the fundamental nature of mind in the following way. The mind's quality of being in essence empty corresponds to the Dharmakaya. Its clear nature corresponds to the Sambhogakaya, and its quality of unimpeded manifestation corresponds to the Nirmanakaya. These qualities, which express the basic nature of mind, are what we term Buddhahood, which is also called "the embodiment of the Three Kayas."

The Dharmakaya, or ultimate aspect, is described in a number of ways. For example, there are traditional references to the Twenty-one Flawless Aspects of the Dharmakaya that represent a state of mind not subject to change or degeneration. There is an omnipresent aspect, in that the Dharmakaya pervades both samsara and Nirvana. There is also the permanent quality, because the Dharmakaya is beyond form, beyond all limiting characteristics, and has no origination or cessation; being beyond dualistic or conceptual frameworks, it is without highness, lowness, happiness, sadness, or any kind of change. In such ways the texts attempt to describe the

Dharmakaya's unchangeable nature, subject neither to degeneration, exhaustion, nor impairment.

The Sambhogakaya is also described from various viewpoints, and most commonly in terms of the Five Certainties. The first of these concerns the form encountered at the Sambhogakaya level. Here, the form of the Teacher has a permanent quality; it has no origin and no end, and therefore differs from all phenomena that are subject to change — differs even from the form in this world of the Buddha Shakyamuni, who took birth, grew old and died. Secondly, although we have a localized perception and speak of particular Buddhas and Buddha-realms, there is, nevertheless, an eternal quality to the environment of the Sambhogakaya that is not subject to change, degeneration or impairment. Thirdly, the transmission of teachings at the Sambhogakaya level of Enlightenment is always that of the Mahayana or Vajrayana. The unending continuity of this teaching is the third certainty. The fourth certainty concerns the retinue or audience of these teachings, which is always composed of beings on the eighth, ninth and tenth Bodhisattva levels, the three highest, purest levels of realization. Finally, there is the certainty of time, the fact that the Sambhogakaya is not subject to normal temporal limitations. These Five Certainties, pertaining to teacher, environment, Doctrine, entourage, and temporal mode, all belong to the level of Pure Form and such form is permanent.

It has been said that the mind is in essence empty and by nature clear, and that there is a third quality, unimpededness, which we experience in our present state as all the emotions, thoughts, concepts, experiences of pleasure and pain, and so forth, which arise without obstruction in our minds. All these are the unimpeded manifestation of mind in the unenlightened context. From the enlightened point of view, however, this unimpeded manifestation is termed the Nirmanakaya: the manifestation of Enlightenment in physical form in the physical world. Various levels and aspects of this phenomenon are described. For example, we can speak of supreme Nirmanakayas, such as the completely enlightened Shakyamuni Buddha, and we can speak of what are termed literally, "birth incarnations" — beings who, although not completely enlightened, nevertheless represent some degree of Enlightenment working through physical form or through various arts, crafts, sciences and so forth. The physical manifestation of Enlightenment is not a deliberate undertaking on the part of the Buddha nature; it is not the result of some determination like "Now I will emanate in this particular realm in this particular form;" rather, it is a spontaneous expression, just as light radiates spontaneously from the sun without the sun issuing directives or giving any conscious thought to the matter. The sun is, and it radiates. Dharmakaya and Sambhogakaya simply are; they radiate, and the radiation is the Nirmanakaya.

Hinayana and Mahayana Views of the Path

What has so far been described as the Truth of the Path pertains equally to Hinayana and Mahayana: At both levels of teaching we find the same concepts of the Five Paths, the Thirty-seven Elements conducive to Enlightenment, and so forth. The difference lies in the scope of the interpretation of these topics. For example, from the Hinayana point of view, generosity involves giving up all one's wealth and, ideally, taking monk's or nun's vows, leading an extremely simple life, with only robes and a begging bowl, and getting only what is necessary for the present day, and no more. In short, the Hinayana ideal of generosity involves a complete rejection of acquisition, a total abandonment of one's attachment to wealth, and the pursuit of a very simplified way of life. From the Mahayana point of view, this ideal is extended to include a continual sharing of whatever wealth comes our way; even our own body is considered worthy as an offering. In one way or another, whatever appears is continually dedicated, either to the Dharma or to the benefit of other beings.

From the Hinayana point of view, morality means very much what we might normally think — living a good life by avoiding harmful or negative actions. This view of morality is also found in the Mahayana, but it is greatly expanded through the emphasis on developing good qualities and virtuous tendencies in ourselves, and by the dedication of our lives for the benefit of other beings. In this way, the scope is greater.

The Hinayana and Mahayana do share views of the Path to Enlightenment but what has been said here about Enlightenment itself pertains particularly to the Mahayana and Vajrayana. For the Hinayana, the goal is the cessation of negative factors; only at the Mahayana and Vajrayana levels does one speak of the development of the mind's positive potential.

We can get a clearer idea of the difference between the two views of Enlightenment by examining the words used to describe it in each system. The Hinayana goal is the attainment of the level of an Arhat. This term is translated into Tibetan as *dra chom pa* [dgra bcom pa], which means "having conquered the enemy." The enemy here is the emotions and the ignorance which keep us locked in samsara, and the intention is to overcome or eliminate those factors. This is where the principle of Cessation—the other term used to describe Enlightenment in the Hinayana—comes in. Cessation refers to stopping the emotions that confuse the mind, and stopping discursive thoughts—fixations on materiality and immateriality, reality and non-reality, and all such conceptual frameworks—that limit awareness. When Cessation is achieved, all of these have been arrested, and the mind is simply absorbed in the experience of Emptiness, without any wavering or distraction. This is the Hinayana ideal, and it will certainly lead to complete Enlightenment. However, the length of time it will take to do so is immense, and during this almost interminable period, there is virtually no ability to help others. That is why the term Hinayana, "the lesser vehicle," is applied, because the scope is relatively narrow. Cessation does, however, represent at least a degree of Liberation from samsara, because an individual who experiences it has no need to reincarnate: the power of karma to cause rebirth in the cycle of samsara has been transcended.

Perhaps the understanding of all these concepts—the Five Paths, the Ten Levels of Bodhisattva Realization, the Thirty-seven Elements conducive to their realization, the different qualities of the Three Kayas—is not strictly necessary; if we are diligent in Dharma practice and meditate, we are going to experience them all anyway. They will not fail to arise just because we don't know what to call them, or necessarily arise just because we do. On the other hand, there seems to be something very important in giving guidelines to help people understand more about the elements of Dharma practice and the enlightened state towards which they're working.

Reasons to Study the Four Noble Truths

The value of understanding our situation from the point of view of both samsara and Nirvana is this: to understand the cause and result of samsara motivates us to seek an alternative: once we have realized the limitations of our situation, there is the possibility of seeking something else. And if we understand the cause and result aspects of the Path, then this fuels our motivation not simply to reject samsara, but to seek Enlightenment. Moreover, to understand the great qualities of Buddhas and Bodhisattvas inspires one with faith in, and awe at, what is possible. Faith, energy, and motivation are very helpful in developing an understanding of the Four Noble Truths.

Having achieved this precious human existence with its opportunities and freedoms, and in having met with the teachings of the Dharma, we are pivotally poised. On one side is the possibility of continuing to wander ignorantly in the cycle of rebirth, and on the other the possibility of transcending samsara and actually achieving Enlightenment. Both possibilities stem from the mind that each and every one of us has and experiences. It is this mind we already have that is essentially empty and illuminating by nature, that can and does experience the different levels of Bodhisattva Realization; it is this same mind that can achieve and experience complete Enlightenment.

3

The Four Dharmas of Gampopa

Our precious human birth affords opportunity and leisure for Dharma practice and gives us access to the vast and profound tradition of the teachings of the Buddhadharma. Among these, the Four Dharmas of Gampopa provide a concise survey of the entire Path, divided into four levels.

The First Dharma: The Mind Turns Towards Dharma

This first teaching involves a thorough understanding of our situation in samsara and the different destinies within the cycle, the six states of rebirth: three lower ones—the hell realms, the hungry ghost realm, and the animal realm; and three higher—the human, *asura*, and god realms. Through this teaching, we learn the consequences of virtuous and unvirtuous actions, which tendencies lead to these various rebirths, and the sufferings which the beings in these realms undergo. We come to understand that although a particular karmic process may lead from higher to lower or lower to higher rebirths, samsara itself provides no means of escape, and if we rely on it, we can make no progress towards Enlightenment. At the beginning of the Path, this understanding of samsara is necessary to turn the mind towards the Dharma, and to do this we contemplate the Four Ordinary Preliminaries.

The first of these concerns the unique value of the human life we are now experiencing. Because of the blessing of the Three Jewels and their influence in previous lives, we have, at some point, developed a virtuous tendency that has brought about our present human birth, with all its opportunities, leisure and freedom to practice Dharma. Very few beings preserve this virtuous tendency (by avoiding negative actions, thoughts, and speech and encouraging positive ones), and very few achieve the resultant state of a precious human birth. If we think of the stars in the night sky as representing the multitude of beings in samsara, then a star in daytime represents the precious human birth—it is something possible, but most unlikely. Human birth is an extremely rare occurrence.

The second of the Four Preliminaries concerns impermanence. Now that we have the precious opportunity of human birth we should make the best use of it and actually realize the full potential of being human. This can be accomplished through our efforts to transcend completely the cycle of rebirth and achieve Buddhahood. In addition we must understand that mortality and impermanence are part of our existence, and that our human birth, obtained with such difficulty, will pass away. In everything we experience, there is moment-by-moment change and instability. Like a candle flame blown by a strong wind, our human existence may be extinguished at any moment; like a bubble on the surface of water, it may suddenly burst; like morning dew on the grass, it soon evaporates.

Next, to realize the full potential of being human, we must examine the concept of karma, the process of cause and effect, especially the relationship between our actions and their results. We need to recognize fully the unfailing connection between what we do now and what we experience later.

The fourth contemplation that turns the mind towards Dharma deals with the unsatisfactory and painful nature of samsara. Without an appreciation of impermanence and our own impending death, we are likely to be distracted by the pleasures of the world and indulge ourselves in emotional conflict and confusion. When that happens, we become exhausted by the life we lead and do not get to what really matters. We neither really see what is actually happening in our lives, nor make good use of our situation. Before we know it, our life is finished and it is time to die. If we lack the foundation of a stable practice, we go to death helplessly, in fear and anguish.

By contemplating these preliminaries — the potential of a precious human existence, impermanence and the inevitability of death, the karmic process of cause and effect, and the sufferings and limitations of samsara — we turn our minds to the Dharma, and thus fulfil the first of the Four Teachings of Gampopa.

The Second Dharma: The Dharma Becomes The Path

Once involved in the teachings, we come to the second of the Four Dharmas: the teachings of the Dharma become our way of life, our path. Our attitude towards what is superior to us — the Three Jewels — begins to change, and so does our attitude towards the beings in samsara who are equal or inferior to us. The first attitude is expressed when we take Refuge, with faith, devotion and respect, in the Buddha, the Dharma and the Sangha. We realize that in Buddhahood one is omniscient and omnipresent, endowed with infinite capabilities. We see that the teachings of the Dharma, which proceed from this enlightened state, are the Path that every being can follow to Enlightenment. We recognize that the Sangha, or assembly of practitioners who realize and transmit the teachings, are companions or guides who can show us the Path. In the Vajrayana tradition, we add the Three Roots — Lama, Yidam and Dharma Protector — to the Three Jewels as sources of Refuge.

When the Dharma becomes our Path, we develop a second attitude, that of compassion. In contemplating the beings who are in samsara with us, we consider that space is infinite, pervading all directions, and that the realm of sentient beings extends as far as space itself. At some point in the past, every one of these numberless beings has been our mother or our father. Through innumerable cycles of lifetimes we have developed an extremely close karmic connection with each one of them. When compassion develops we see that all life is the same, and that every single being wishes to be happy: in every form of life a fundamental search for happiness goes on—but in a way that contradicts and defeats the aim of this search. Few beings understand that real happiness is the result of virtuous conduct. Many are involved in actually destroying their chances for happiness through confused and harmful actions and thoughts. When we see this we develop real affection and compassion for other beings. This infinite compassion for all forms of life is the second attitude involved in making the teaching our Path. Through faith and compassion the teaching that has attracted us becomes an entire way of life.

The Development of Compassion

Although we realize the necessity of working not only for our own benefit but for the welfare of all beings, we need to be honest about our own limitations and recognize that we have little power or ability to be truly effective in helping beings to free themselves. The way we become effective in this is through achieving Buddhahood or, at least, by reaching some level of Bodhisattva realization. At these higher levels we gain the ability to manifest for the sake of guiding beings out of their confusion.

The attitude of altruism is called Relative Bodhicitta; the desire to develop it is the foundation of Mahayana practice and the vessel for all virtue.

One method for developing Bodhicitta is called tong len [gtong len], which literally means "sending [and] taking." The attitude here is that each of us is only one being, while the number of beings in the universe is infinite. Would it not be a worthy goal if this one being could take on all the pain of every other being in the universe and free each and every one of them from suffering? We therefore resolve to take on ourselves all this suffering, to take it away from all other beings, even their incipient or potential suffering, and all of its causes. At the same time we develop the attitude of sending all our virtue, happiness, health, wealth and potential for long life to other beings. Anything that we enjoy, anything noble or worthy, positive or happy in our situation we send selflessly to every other being. Thus the meditation is one of willingly taking on all that is negative and willingly giving away all that is positive. We reverse our usual tendency to cling to what we want for ourselves and to ignore others.

We develop a deep empathy with everything that lives. The method of sending and taking is a most effective way of developing the Bodhisattva's motivation.

The kind of compassion we have described so far is called "compassion with reference to sentient beings" (sem chen la mik pay nying je [sems can la dmigs pa'i snying rje]). A dualism lingers here, however, because we are still caught by the threefold idea of (1) ourselves experiencing the compassion, (2) other beings as the objects of compassion, and (3) the actual act of feeling compassion through understanding or perceiving the suffering of others. This framework prepares our path in the Mahayana. Once this kind of compassion has been established, we arrive at a second. The realization begins to grow that the self which is feeling the compassion, the objects of the compassion, and the compassion itself are all in a certain sense illusory. We see that these three aspects belong to a conventional, not ultimate, reality. They are nothing in themselves, but simply illusions that create the appearance of a dualistic framework. Perceiving these illusions and thereby understanding the true emptiness of all phenomena and experience is what we call "compassion with reference to all phenomena" (chö la mik pay nying je [chos la dmigs pa'i snying rje]). This is the main path of Mahayana practice.

From this second kind of compassion a third develops, "non-referential compassion" (mi me nying je [dmigs med snying rje]). Here we entirely transcend any concern with subject/object reference. It is the ultimate experience that results in Buddhahood. All these three levels of compassion are connected, so if we begin with the basic level by developing loving-kindness and compassion towards all beings, we lay a foundation which guarantees that our path will lead directly to Enlightenment.

The Third Dharma: The Path Dispels Confusion

The third Dharma of Gampopa states that by traveling the Path our confusion is dispelled. The principal theme of the teaching here is the experience of emptiness — the realization of the ultimate nature of mind. In meditation we realize that our mind and all the experiences which it projects are fundamentally unreal: they exist conventionally, but not in an ultimate sense. This Realization of Emptiness is known as Ultimate Bodhicitta.

An analogy can be drawn between the ocean and the mind, which is essentially empty, without limiting characteristics or ultimate reality. This empty mind, however, has its projection, which is the whole phenomenal world. The form, sound, taste, touch, smell, and inner thoughts, which constitute what we experience correspond to waves on the surface of the ocean. Once we see, through meditation, that the nature of mind is fundamentally empty, we become automatically aware that the projections of mind are fundamentally empty too. These projections are like waves that arise from and subside into the ocean; at no point are they ever separate from it.

Although we may have some understanding that mind is essentially empty, it may be difficult to relate this idea to phenomenal existence. An example may help. At the present moment we have a physical body, and during our waking existence we are extremely attached to it. We take it to be real, a self-existent entity. But during dreams, we inhabit a different kind of body, and experience a different state of being. A complete phenomenal existence is associated with this "dream body." We see, smell, touch, hear, feel, think and communicate—we experience a complete universe. But when we awaken it becomes obvious that the universe of the dream has no ultimate reality. It certainly is not in the outer world as we know it, nor in the room where we sleep, nor inside our body; it cannot be found anywhere. When the dream is over, its 'reality' simply disappears—it was only a projection of mind. It is fairly easy to understand this in relation to the dream state. What we must also comprehend is that our experience in the waking state is of the same general nature and occurs through the same process.

Realized Mahasiddhas, such as Tilopa and Naropa of India, or Marpa and Milarepa of Tibet, were able to perform miraculous changes in the phenomenal universe. They could do so because they had realized the entire phenomenal world as essentially empty and a projection of mind. This allowed them to manifest miracles and actually change the phenomenal world. Such transformation is not possible when our mind clings to what we experience as ultimately real and immutable.

The present phase of our existence ends in death, when the karma which directs the course of this physical existence is exhausted.

At death there is a definite and final separation of consciousness from the physical body, which is simply discarded. What continues is the individual consciousness, the mind of the being entering into the bardo experience. During that after-death state, we experience another kind of phenomenal universe. Though lacking the basis of a physical organism, the mind is able to see, hear, smell, taste, touch, think, and perceive in much the same way as it does now. Though there is nothing more than a state of consciousness, the mind continues to follow its habits and to manifest in set patterns. Thus our habitual conviction that experience is ultimately real continues after physical death, and what happens there resembles what happens in the dream state and waking consciousness.

A story about a monk in Tibet illustrates this. It happened not very long ago, in fact, during the lifetime of my father. Near my home in Tibet there is a Nyingmapa monastery called Dzokchen. A monk from this monastery decided that he did not want to stay there any more, but preferred to go into business. He left and went to the north of that region to become a trader, hoping to accumulate a fortune. He actually did become fairly successful. Because of his former relationship with a monastery, he was also considered something of a Dharma teacher, so he had a group of followers as well as the wealth amassed through his trading ventures. One day he met a magician who was able to exercise a certain mental control over people. The trader didn't realize the power of this person, and the magician cast a spell that caused the trader to experience a powerful illusion in which he met a woman, married and had children; he acquired a large estate and family to look after, and engaged in many trading ventures that brought him vast riches. He passed his whole life this way and became old with white hair and few teeth. Then the illusion disappeared: he was back where he had been, and perhaps only one or two days had passed. During that time the magician had stolen everything he possessed, and the trader woke without a penny in the world. He had only the memory of his long fantasy of a lifetime's activities, distractions and projects.

Just like the trader's fantasy, our own daily experiences have an illusory quality. In the Mahayana sutras, it is taught that everything we experience is like a reflection, a mirage, a rainbow in the sky, or the moon shining on the water's surface; everything we experience has only conventional reality and is ultimately unreal.

We experience the third Dharma of Gampopa when, first, we become convinced that we must dispel our confusion through understanding and experiencing the essential emptiness of mind, and, second, when this reveals the illusory nature of all phenomena; then the Path dispels confusion.

The Fourth Dharma:
Confusion Arises as Primordial Awareness

The fourth Dharma of Gampopa is the transformation of confusion into Primordial Awareness. This fundamental transformation is effected on the level of Anuttarayogatantra, the highest of the four levels of Vajrayana teachings.

This transformation is not difficult to explain theoretically. In an ordinary state awareness is clouded and confused; if we recognize the mind's nature, then we experience Primordial Awareness. On a practical level, however, this does not happen automatically: a certain kind of skillful means is needed. To transform discursive into enlightened awareness, we use the wealth of techniques available in the Vajrayana, especially the Development and Fulfillment stages of meditation (che rim/dzo rim [(bskyed rim/rdzogs rim]). In our present situation as unenlightened beings, our three faculties of body, speech, and mind are obscured by basic ignorance. To transform that confusion into awareness, we must become physically, verbally, and mentally aware, so in Vajrayana practice we utilize these very faculties of our whole being to effect a complete transformation.

Considering our physical body, we can see how we are attached to it as something permanent, pure and real. Yet this physical body is temporary, composed of numerous impure and decaying substances. It is conventionally, not ultimately, real. Our habitual and instinctive clinging to it obstructs the arising of Primordial Awareness. We must come to realize that this body is simply something that appears and that it has no self-nature. Based on the projections of the mind, the body represents the heart of the form aspect of consciousness. Until we realize this, the transformation of confusion into Primordial Awareness will not happen spontaneously or easily.

In tantric practice, the body is transformed by a meditation that leads us to identify with a pure or enlightened form, for exam-

ple, Chenrezi, the Bodhisattva of Compassion. Here we put aside
the fixation on our own body and instead identify with a pure form.
In doing so, it is important also to realize that the deity is pure appearance, and does not partake of substantiality in any way. In
meditation we become completely identified with this form, which is
empty, without solidity, without self-nature or ultimate reality
beyond its pure appearance. This experience is called "The Union
of Appearance and Emptiness" (nang tong sung juk [snang stong
zung 'jug]).

Such a transformation is based upon understanding that all our
experience is a subjective projection of mind, and therefore our attitude towards things is decisive. Through changing our attitude we
change our experience, and when we meditate in the way described,
transformation is possible. This is especially true when we focus on
an enlightened form such as the Bodhisattva of Compassion. The
image of Chenrezi itself is a real expression of the state of enlightened compassion. It is not a fabrication. There is actually an
enlightened being called Chenrezi, able to confer blessing and attainment. To experience this, certain conditions must come
together. An analogy would be taking a photograph of someone.
We put film in the camera, we point it at whomever we're
photographing and take the picture; the image of the person is projected onto the film, and when it's developed, we have a certain image of that person. Something similar happens when we meditate on
an enlightened form. There is an "external" expression called
Chenrezi. Through our efforts in meditation, we come to identify
with this pure form, to have faith in it, and to realize the intrinsic
compassion and state of awareness Chenrezi represents. In this way
we can become a "copy" of the deity and receive the blessing of the
Bodhisattva of Compassion. This is the first aspect of the transformation of confusion into Primordial Awareness based on meditation
upon our body as an enlightened form.

The second aspect of transformation concerns our speech.
Although it may be easy to consider speech as intangible, that it
simply appears and disappears, we actually relate to it as to
something real. It is because we become so attached to what we say
and hear that speech has such power. Mere words, which have no
ultimate reality, can determine our happiness and suffering. We

create pleasure and pain through our fundamental clinging to sound and speech.

In the Vajrayana context, we recite and meditate on mantra, which is enlightened sound, the speech of the deity, the Union of Sound and Emptiness (dra tong sung juk [sgra stong zung 'jug]). It has no intrinsic reality, but is simply the manifestation of pure sound, experienced simultaneously with its Emptiness. Through mantra, we no longer cling to the reality of the speech and sound encountered in life, but experience it as essentially empty. Then confusion of the speech aspect of our being is transformed into enlightened awareness.

At first, the Union of Sound and Emptiness is simply an intellectual concept of what our meditation should be. Through continued application, it becomes our actual experience. Here, as elsewhere in the practice, attitude is all-important, as this story about a teacher in Tibet illustrates. The teacher had two disciples, who both undertook to perform a hundred million recitations of the mantra of Chenrezi, OM MANI PADME HUNG. In the presence of their Lama, they took a vow to do so, and went off to complete the practice. One of the disciples was very diligent, though his realization was perhaps not so profound. He set out to accomplish the practice as quickly as possible and recited the mantra incessantly, day and night. After long efforts, he completed his one hundred million recitations, in three years. The other disciple was extremely intelligent, but perhaps not as diligent, because he certainly did not launch into the practice with the same enthusiasm. But when his friend was approaching the completion of his retreat, the second disciple, who still had not recited very many mantras, went up on the top of a hill. He sat down there, and began to meditate that all beings throughout the universe were transformed into Chenrezi. He meditated that the sound of the mantra was not only issuing from the mouth of each and every being, but that every atom in the universe was vibrating with it, and for a few days he recited the mantra in this state of samadhi.

When the two disciples went to their Lama to indicate they they'd finished the practice, he said, "Oh, you've both done excellently. You were very diligent, and *you* were very wise. You both accomplished the one hundred million recitations of the mantra."

Thus through changing our attitude and developing our understanding, practice becomes far more powerful.

The six syllable mantra of Chenrezi, OM MANI PADME HUNG, is an expression of Chenrezi's blessing and enlightened power. The six syllables are associated with different aspects of our experience: six basic emotional afflictions in the mind are being transformed, six aspects of Primordial Awareness are being realized. These sets of six belong to the mandala of the six different Buddha families which become manifest in the enlightened mind. The mantra of Chenrezi has power to effect transformations on all these levels.

Another way of interpreting the mantra is that the syllable OM is the essence of enlightened form; MANI PADME, the four syllables in the middle, represent the speech of Enlightenment; and the last syllable HUNG represents the mind of Enlightenment. The body, speech, and mind of all Buddhas and Bodhisattvas are inherent in the sound of this mantra. It purifies the obscurations of body, speech, and mind, and brings all beings to the state of Realization. When it is joined with our own faith and efforts in meditation and recitation, the transformative power of the mantra arises and develops. It is truly possible to purify ourselves in this way.

The mind aspect of the Chenrezi meditation centers in the heart region where the mantra and seed-syllable HRĪH are located. Light is visualized as going out from these and making offerings to all the Buddhas, purifying the obscurations of all beings, and establishing them in Enlightenment. The mind aspect is also connected with formless meditation, simply resting the mind in its own empty nature. After practicing this for some time, a change will occur: we will have the experience that anything arising in the mind, any emotion or thought, arises from and dissolves back into Emptiness. For that duration we are nowhere other than in Emptiness. In this state, we experience mind as the Union of Awareness and Emptiness (rik tong sung juk [rig stong zung 'jug]). This is Mahāmudrā.

The threefold Chenrezi meditation thus utilizes meditational techniques relating to body, speech, and mind. At the end of a session of practice, the visualization dissolves into a formless state, and we simply rest the mind evenly in its own nature. At this time we can experience body, speech, and mind as arising from basic, empty mind. We recognize this mind as the fundamental aspect and body and speech to be secondary projections based upon consciousness. This represents the gathering of all aspects of our experience into one—the Emptiness of mind from which everything arises. Through this, we have realized the fourth Dharma of Gampopa: confusion has arisen as Primordial Awareness.

4

Bardo

The word bardo literally means "an interval between two things." *Bar* means 'interval' and *do* means 'two.' We can think of this interval in a spatial or temporal way. If there are two houses, the space between them is a bardo. The period between sunrise and sunset, the interval of daylight, is a bardo. A bardo can be of long or short duration, of wide or narrow expanse.

To a large extent our experience is made up of intervals between one thing and another. Even in the case of the momentary thoughts that arise in our mind, there is an interval between one thought arising and fading and the next thought appearing. Such a gap, even if infinitesimal, is a part of every process. Everything we experience has this quality of intervals between states.

The Six Bardos

Certain aspects of bardo are more important than others. One of the most crucial is our waking existence, from the moment of birth to the time we die. This waking existence is the first great bardo in our experience, the Bardo between Birth and Death (che shi bar do [skye shi'i bar do]).

The bardo of the dream state, which lasts from the moment we go to sleep at night until the moment we wake in the morning is another example. The state of consciousness that obtains during that interval is termed the Dream Bardo (mi lam bar do [rmi lam bar do]).

For an ordinary person, the trauma of death produces a state of unconsciousness, which lasts for an indefinite time: it may be very brief or quite long. Traditionally, this period of blackout is considered to last three and a half days. Afterwards, the consciousness of the individual begins to awaken again and experience things in a new way. The interval of unconsciousness into which the mind is plunged by the trauma of death, and which lasts till the awakening of consciousness again, is referred to in Tibetan as the *chö nyi bardo* [chos nyid bar do], the interval of the ultimate nature of phenomena; here the mind is plunged into its own nature, though in a confused or ignorant way.

The next phase of the after-death experience is the reawakening of consciousness, which includes the many days that can be spent experiencing the fantastic projections of mind, the hallucinations produced and experienced by the mind in the after-death state. From the moment of this reawakening of consciousness (the end of the *chö nyi* bardo) to the moment we take actual physical rebirth in one of the six realms of samsara, is known as the *si pa bardo* [srid pa bardo], the Bardo of Becoming. Another way of interpreting the Tibetan is as the bardo of possibility, since at this point we have not taken physical birth and there are numerous possibilities for various kinds of existence.

These are the four major instances of the Bardo principle. Another example is a state of meditation: when someone who practices begins to meditate effectively, there is a certain change in consciousness; when that person rises from the meditation and goes about worldly activities again, there is a cessation of that state of consciousness. The interval of actual formal meditation is called the Bardo of Meditative Stability, *sam ten bar do* [bsam gtan bar do]. The sixth bardo we distinguish is the Bardo of Gestation, *che nay bar do* [skye gnas bar do]. This interval begins at the end of the Bardo of Becoming when the consciousness of the being unites with the sperm and egg in the womb of the mother and lasts until the time of physical birth, the beginning of the Bardo between Birth and Death.

These six kinds of bardo that we experience as human or sentient beings in samsara can be changed for the better, but the power to do this lies in the waking state. It is in the bardo of our present lives that we can make the most progress in developing the ability to deal effectively with all the others. What we usually mean by the word, bardo, however, is the Bardo of Becoming, the phase of hallucinations before new physical conception.

The Five Elements and the Nature of Mind

Our present unenlightened state is based on a fundamental state of ignorance, a fundamental discursive consciousness, *kun shi nam she* [kun gzhi rnam shes]. It is the fundamental consciousness which is distorted and confused. There is, however, a possibility of experiencing the true nature of mind, and when that pure awareness is present we no longer have *kun shi nam she* but *kun shi ye she* [kun gzhi ye shes]. That change of a single syllable from *nam* to *ye*, makes a tremendous difference, because now we are referring to fundamental Primordial Awareness rather than fundamental ignorance.

In both cases we are talking about mind, which essentially embodies what in our physical universe we term the five elements. The potential for these elements exists in the mind and always has—it is not something created at some particular time. In its inherent nature, mind always has the five elemental qualities, and it is from this potential that the experiences of the after-death state arise.

When we speak of mind, we speak of something that is not a thing in itself. In its most fundamental sense, mind is not something we can limit. We cannot say it has a particular shape, size or location, color or form, or any other limiting characteristic. The element we call space, which in our perceptual situation also has no limiting characteristics, is this very emptiness of mind; this is the elemental quality of space in the mind.

But mind is not simply empty; it has the illuminating potential to perceive anything whatsoever. This unlimited ability of mind to perceive is its illuminating nature, and corresponds to the element of fire.

This mind, essentially empty and illuminating, gives rise to all experience which, whether of samsara or Nirvana, is rooted in mind just as plants are rooted in soil. This function of the mind as the origin of all experience corresponds to the elemental quality of earth.

Another aspect of the mind is its dynamic quality. Mind is never still: no single experience in it lasts, but quickly passes to another. Whether one is undergoing an emotional reaction, an experience of pleasure or pain, or a sensory perception such as seeing or hearing, the contents of the mind are always in a state of flux. This continual activity of mind is the elemental quality of wind.

Mind with these four elemental qualities has always been so and always will be. This very continuity, and the fact that mind adapts itself to different situations, corresponds to the element of water. Just as water sustains its continuity and adapts itself to every contour as it flows, the mind too is fluent, continuous, and adaptable.

The Five Elements and the Physical Body

The origin or basis of all experience is mind, characterized by the five elemental qualities. Our particular situation at the moment is that of physical waking existence, in which we experience what is termed the body of Completely Ripened Karma (nam min ji lü [rnam smin gyi lus]). The meaning here is that completely ripened karmic tendencies have given rise to this seemingly solid, concrete projection of mind that is our physical body.

The connection between the body we now experience and the mind which produced it is as follows. The solid elements of our body, such as flesh and bone, represent the element of earth, just as the "solidity" of mind—its function as the basis and origin of all experience—reflects the element of earth. Similarly, the bodily fluids such as blood, saliva, urine, lymph and so forth, represent the element of water. The biological warmth of the body is the element of fire, while the element of space is represented by the orifices of the body, and by the spatial separation of the organs, which, instead of forming a homogeneous mass, are distinct and separate from each other. Finally, there is the element of wind, which is connected with the breath, and maintains the organism by way of the respiratory process.

In short, it is from mind, which embodies the five elemental qualities, that the physical body develops. The physical body itself is imbued with these qualities, and it is because of this mind/body complex that we perceive the outside world — which in turn is composed of the five elemental qualities of earth, water, fire, wind, and space.

The Five Elements in the Bardo

Right now we are at a pivotal point between impure, unenlightened states of existence and the possibility of enlightenment. For ordinary beings the *chö nyi* bardo is experienced as a period of deep unconsciousness following the moment of death. There is no mental activity or perception, only a blank state of fundamental unconsciousness. This bardo ends with the first glimmer of awareness in the mind. In the interval between the end of the *chö nyi* bardo and before the beginning of the *si pa* bardo there arises what is called the Vision of the Five Lights. The appearance of these is connected with the five elemental qualities.

The different colors which the mind in the bardo state perceives are the natural expression, the radiance, of the fundamental, intrinsic qualities of mind. The element of water is perceived as white light; space as blue light; earth as yellow; fire as red; and wind as green. These colors are simply the natural expression of the elemental qualities in the mind when the first glimmer of consciousness begins to appear.

As consciousness begins to develop and perceive more, the experience of the elemental qualities also becomes more developed. What was formerly the simple impression of diferent rays or colors of light now undergoes a change. The light begins to integrate itself and cohere into *tig le* [thig le], points or balls of light in varying sizes. It is within these spheres of concentrated light that we experience the Mandalas of the Peaceful and Wrathful Deities.

In this context we speak of the five realms of existence in any one of which we may be reborn, because of the impure level of our experience. The usual description is of the six realms of existence, the six principal emotions that lead to them, and the six Buddhas who appear in them. In the context of the five-fold mandala pattern, however, desire and avarice are combined, because they share the same basic nature of clinging, and so the realm of the *asuras* is eliminated, the higher *asuras* being re-classified with desire gods in the god realm, and the lower *asuras* included in the animal realm.

The Mandalas of the Peaceful and Wrathful Deities

From an absolute level, the mind that perceives a deity and the deity itself are not two separate things, but are essentially the same. As long as we have no direct realization, however, the mind has the impression of being an "I" which experiences and takes as "other" that which is experienced. During the after-death experience, this split results in a tendency of the mind to feel threatened when the first mandala of the peaceful deities arises: the Mandala of the Five Buddha Families, their consorts and attendant deities, and a sixth family, that of Dorje Sempa, like a canopy over the whole mandala. At this time, we perceive enormous spherical concentrations of light, in which we see the Mandala of the Peaceful Deities emanating a most brilliant radiance. To the confused mind, this radiance is quite overpowering, and to confront the Peaceful Deities is rather like trying to stare into the sun. With the peaceful deities, we also simultaneously perceive the six light rays connected with the six realms of samsara. These are far less intense, so the mind that is repelled by the experience of the pure forms tends to be attracted by the subdued light rays leading to the various states of rebirth in samsara. In this way the confused mind is drawn towards samsaric rebirth.

After the mandala of the Peaceful Deities comes the Mandala of the Wrathful Deities. Ignorance again causes the brilliance and power of these forms, spontaneous expressions of the mind's own nature, to be perceived as something external and threatening. At this point the after-death experience becomes terrifying and repellent, instead of an experience of the unity of the perceiver and the perceived.

The Possibility of Enlightenment in the Bardo

The cycle of teachings known in Tibetan as the *Bardo Tödröl* [bar do thos grol] and the empowerments connected with it are designed to help practitioners receive the blessing and develop the understanding that will benefit them in the after-death experience. With this support, when the pure forms are perceived, they will be seen for what they are — projections of mind essentially identical with it and neither external nor threatening. Liberation arises at that moment in the after-death state when consciousness can realize its experiences to be nothing other than mind itself. The teachings and empowerments connected with the *Bardo Tödröl* cycle introduce us to the deities and explanatory concepts and so prepare us for what happens after death.

The possibility of enlightenment in the after death state rests upon three things. The first is the fundamentally enlightened nature of mind, the seed of Buddhahood, without which nothing would be possible. The second is the blessing inherent in the pure forms of the deities. The third is the connection we have established with those deities through empowerment, and the understanding we have, both intellectually and intuitively, of what is actually taking place. When all these three elements come together, the possibility exists of achieving liberation during the instant of confronting the mandalas of the deities.

If this liberation does not happen in the interval between the *chö nyi* bardo and the Bardo of Becoming, the benefits of receiving empowerment and understanding teachings about the nature of the after-death experience continue into the subsequent phases of the after-death experience, that of the Bardo of Becoming. This means that we can either experience a positive rebirth in the cycle of samsara or, in some cases, achieve existence in what we term the Buddha Realms, a great and sure step towards ultimate Enlightenment.

The Bardo of Becoming

The experience of confronting the mandalas of the deities takes place only briefly and if the opportunity is lost, then the mind enters the Bardo of Becoming. Here the situation becomes roughly analogous to what we experience now—many varied impressions continually arise in the mind and we cling to them, taking them all to be ultimately real. This hallucinatory state is traditionally said to last for a period of forty-nine days before the consciousness takes physical form again as an embryo. At the end of each week there is the trauma of realizing that we are dead and our minds plunge into another state of unconsciousness like the one immediately after death, but not quite as intense. After each of these very short periods of unconsciousness, consciousness returns, and once more the mandalas of the deities present themselves, but now in a fragmentary and fleeting way. The successive opportunities afforded by these appearances are not as great as at the first stage, but the possibility of Liberation does recur throughout the after-death experience.

The Symbolism of the Mandala of Deities

The purity of enlightenment is embodied by the mandala of deities. For example, what we normally experience as the five *skandhas* (the aggregates of the mind/body complex) we recognize on the pure level as the Buddhas of the Five Families. The mind's elemental qualities, which we experience as the elements in our physical body and the outer universe, on the pure level are the five female consorts of the five Buddhas. On the ordinary level we experience eight types of confused consciousness, while on the pure level these are eight male Bodhisattvas. On the impure level we speak of the eight objects of those different kinds of consciousness, and on the pure level we speak of the eight female Bodhisattvas. Each one of these pure forms expresses an enlightened perspective of a part of our impure experience. It is not only possible to connect the different aspects of our impure consciousness with the pure forms, but also to connect these pure forms with the nature of mind itself.

There has been and could still be much commentary on the relationship between these different levels of expression and our own experience. For our present purposes, it is sufficient to understand that the six bardos we've discussed briefly are the six major phases of experience for any being wandering in the cycle of rebirth. In every one of them the practice of Dharma is of the greatest possible value, for through it we can purify ourselves of confusion, obscurations, and negative emotions, and further develop our awareness and merit.

Questions and Answers

QUESTION: Aren't the Mandalas of the Peaceful and Wrathful Deities related to one particular cultural tradition? How do those schooled in other traditions perceive them?

ANSWER: In the tradition of these teachings it doesn't matter whether you're a Buddhist or not: you will still have the experience of the wrathful and peaceful deities. The advantage of being a Buddhist or having practiced this particular approach is that you will recognize the experience for what it is. But the experience is fundamentally the same, even for non-humans. Every being that goes through the bardo has some perception of the lights, of the concentrated spheres of light, and the mandalas appearing within them. Usually, however, there is no recognition and no attempt at recognition, just a feeling that the experience is threatening and repellent. The mind is terrified and retreats from the experience.

In the traditional texts it is stated that even the consciousness of an insect in the bardo state has the same experience. Each and every being in the six realms of existence has what is called Tathagatagarbha, the Seed of Enlightenment, which is fundamental awareness of the ultimate nature of mind. It is from this that bardo experiences arise as natural projections of mind, not as something produced by cultural conditioning.

QUESTION: The mind is traditionally described as having three aspects; are the three elements that correspond to these aspects more important than the remaining two?

ANSWER: In the presentation of mind as having three aspects—its essence is empty, its nature is clarity, and its manifestation is unimpeded—we reckon the Emptiness and the Clarity of mind as the elements of space and fire. The element of wind, the continual movement of mind, is the third aspect, unimpeded manifestation. Now the element of earth is the function of mind as the origin and basis of all experience, and the element of water is the continuity of mind. These two functions (continuity and basis) apply to all three aspects. Thus, the mind is essentially empty (space), has Clarity (fire) and the ability to manifest unimpededly (wind), and throughout all three there is continuity (water) and the ability to provide a basis (earth).

QUESTION: I've heard that the body should not be disturbed for three or four days after death. In the West the custom is to embalm the body very soon after death. How important is it that the body be undisturbed, and for how long?

ANSWER:Generally speaking, it's good to leave the corpse undisturbed as long as possible. But in many circumstances this is difficult, because we simply don't have the attitude towards death reflected in the bardo teachings. Once a person has died, we feel that the mind no longer has any need for the corpse. We don't have the same kind of respect for the corpse that Buddhists in Tibet did.

But it's not easy to explain these ideas, and if you simply say, "Don't move or touch the body," without giving any reason, you may only make people angry. On the other hand, perhaps you could explain some of these ideas. People might at least appreciate the importance to you of what you're saying, and since they have some feeling of respect towards the corpse, might do their best not to disturb it. It's hard to tell. The general principle of not disturbing a corpse for a short period after death could be encouraged. It is beneficial.

5

Mandala

The third of the Kagyü Preliminaries (see pages 9–10), the Mandala Offering, is connected with the accumulation of merit and the deepening of awareness. It is similar to other gestures such as placing flowers, incense, or lamps on a shrine as an offering to the Three Jewels. A lay person might give an offering to a monk or a nun to support their practice, or a disciple might give an offering to a Lama. Such offerings accumulate merit for those who make them, and therefore help to deepen their understanding and awareness. The practice of the Mandala Offering, however, is concerned with offering nothing less than the universe. The structure of the meditation presents the whole universe, with everything worthy of offering, whether material or imagined, including, for example, the physical environment, whose natural beauty does not have to be fabricated, but is simply there to be offered. The Mandala Offering integrates all these perceptions into a single meditation. If this is done with an attitude of faith and devotion, the meditator's mind becomes extremely powerful, and the merit and awareness that result are no different from what could result from actually offering the whole universe to the Three Jewels.

Mandala is a Sanskrit word which the Tibetans translated by *chin khor* [khyil 'khor], which means center and circumference. In the Mandala Offering, a center with its surrounding environment forms a complete system, and constitutes an ideal conception of the universe. Its cosmology is based upon the conception of the central mountain, Sumeru, [ri rab] as axis of the universe, with its continents, mountain ranges and so forth, concentrically arrayed.

For the physical offering we use a metal plate on which to heap up grain, perhaps with precious stones mixed in, in a symmetrical pattern on the plate. This is used to focus the mind on the meditation and to provide a support for the very complex visualization of the universe being offered.

The Variety of Cosmologies

This symbolic cosmology disturbs many people in the modern world because they take it to contradict what we experience with our own senses and with the technology we have now developed. These days we have a conception of the universe that includes our solar system and our own realm as a spherical planet turning around the sun. People have evidence of this, and therefore see a discrepancy between the present world view and the world view presented in the Mandala Offering.

Buddhahood is a state of omniscience; from that omniscience the Buddha spoke of this cosmology—but not as the only one. Different beings, because of their different karmic tendencies and different levels of awareness, experience the universe in different ways. So in many of the Buddha's teachings, especially in the vast sutra known as the *Avatamsaka*, various cosmologies are presented. Some involve only a single continent. Others have a multiplicity of worlds, such as the Mandala Offering pattern. Others involve planetary systems, spherical worlds, and so forth. Any one of these various cosmologies is completely valid for the beings whose karmic projections cause them to experience their universe in that way. There is a certain relativity in the way one experiences the world.

This means that all the possible experiences of every being in the six realms of existence, shaping the ways in which each perceives the universe, are based upon karmic inclinations and degrees of individual development. Thus, on a relative level, any cosmology is valid. On an ultimate level no cosmology is absolutely true. It cannot be universally valid, given the different conventional situations of beings.

We have quite a number of people here today. If we all lay down to take a nap and had dreams, and if someone said on waking, "My dream was the only true one. All the rest of you had false dreams," how plausible would we find that? We all have different perceptions based on our individual karmic tendencies.

In order to accumulate merit and develop awareness, it is most effective to offer what is most beautiful. Because of our dualistic clinging, we feel attraction to what we consider good, wholesome or beautiful and aversion to what we consider ugly or disgusting. When we choose what to offer, we should acknowledge that we have this dualistic clinging and only offer what pleases us. Of all the possible cosmologies, the most beautiful, the most pleasing as an object of meditation, seems to be this mandala pattern of the central mountain with four continents. Since we wish to offer only the best, this beautiful model of the universe is used.

Making Pure Offerings

In India, during the time of the Buddha, there was an old couple who were very poor and had only a small plot of land, barely enough to get by. One day they realized they were growing old and were coming closer and closer to death. They felt they should make use of the precious opportunity of being human by performing at least one gesture that would accumulate great merit and develop their awareness before they died. They discussed what particular formal act would be most appropriate. As it happened, Shariputra, one of the wisest of the Buddha's disciples, lived nearby. They decided to invite the Venerable Shariputra to their home and serve him a midday meal as an offering. They would then make prayers of aspiration in his presence to receive this blessing.

The old couple made their preparations, invited Shariputra, offered him the meal, formulated their prayers, and received his blessing. And afterward things went on much as before, except that when the growing season was finished and they went along with everyone else to harvest their rice, they found that all the grains in their small paddy were not rice at all but pure gold.

Soon everyone was talking about the field of golden rice, and the news quickly reached the ears of Ajatasatru, a famous king of Buddhist India. He said to himself, "This is entirely improper. I'm the king, I should have control of that field." He ordered his ministers to confiscate the land from the old couple and to give them another rice paddy of equal size elsewhere. His messengers duly went out, found the old couple, and moved them to another plot of land. But when this had been done, the confiscated grains of gold turned to rice once again, and the rice on the couple's new land became gold. Word of this got back to the king and he said, "Go, do it again. Take the golden rice."

This happened seven times. Each time the messengers took the land from the old couple and gave them another plot, the same change took place; the king was left with rice and the old couple had the gold.

By now people began to wonder why this was happening. They went to see the Buddha and described the situation. The Buddha explained the karmic connection between the meritorious act and the result the old couple were experiencing even in the same lifetime. The event became a famous example of the unfailing nature of the karmic process. It did a great deal to establish people's understanding of karma as a factor in all that happens, and revealed the connection between what is done and what is experienced.

The old couple's action was extremely meritorious for two reasons. First, the object of their respect and devotion was Shariputra, an extremely pure and holy being. This is what is technically termed the "field." If the object of our devotion and offerings, the field upon which we are working, is a pure one, it is very fertile in blessings. The second reason was the couple's pure motivation in making the offering out of respect and faith. The double purity of field and motivation made the offering powerful and great merit was accumulated.

In the case of the Mandala Offering, these elements are at work as well: what is chosen as the field, the object of our offerings, is the Three Jewels, which are completely pure and embody inconceivable blessing, and our own pure motivation in making the offering to develop merit and perfect awareness. It is the coming together of these circumstances that make the practice so effective.

With reference to the merit involved, the Buddha said that the wish to offer the mandala (to say nothing of actually offering it) or making the offering plate used during the practice, if done properly, would accumulate merit that would give dominion over the world.

Now all of you are intelligent people, and no doubt it has occured to you that there seems to be a difference between the formal Mandala Offering — piling rice on a plate — and what the old couple offered to Shariputra, which was almost everything they had. Indeed, you may feel that there is a fundamental difference between these two kinds of offering. But there isn't. There is actually a great similarity between them, and the link is our motivation.

The Importance of Motivation

During the Buddha's lifetime there lived in India a Buddhist king who planned to sponsor an assembly wherein the Buddha and five hundred of his disciples, all realized Arhats, would spend the three months of the summer retreat. The king would provide them with a park to stay in and offer them all the food and clothing they needed. When the Buddha came to stay in this grove with his disciples, it was their daily custom to dedicate the merit of their activity for the benefit of all beings. Following the midday meal the Buddha would recite a prayer to this effect: "May all the virtue and merit achieved by the King through sponsoring this summer retreat be shared for the benefit of all sentient beings."

Now there was an old beggar woman who lived in the town. Though poverty-stricken, she had a wholesome frame of mind; when she saw the king undertaking this project, she thought to herself, "Wonderful! Here is a man who because of his previous accumulation of merit has a fortunate rebirth as a powerful king. Now he's utilizing that opportunity to render service to Buddha and his attendants. He is ensuring continuous accumulation of merit, development of awareness, and definite progress on the path to Liberation. How wonderful this is!" The old beggar woman was truly thankful and glad to see the king undertaking this virtuous work; she had a deep sense of joy that someone was accumulating such merit.

One day after the midday meal, the Buddha turned to the king and said, "Your majesty, should I share the merit as usual using your name, or should I insert the name of someone who has more merit than you?" The king thought to himself, "What's he talking about? There can't be anyone with more merit than I." So he said, "Your Reverence, if in fact there is a person with more merit than I, then please by all means share the merit on their behalf." So the Buddha proceeded to dedicate the merit accumulated by this old beggar woman for the benefit of all sentient beings. This went on for a number of days. Every day the Buddha would use the name of the beggar woman instead of the king's name, and the king grew depressed.

The king's ministers now began discussing how to cheer him up. One of them, who was very bright and rather crafty, thought of a plan. He organized an offering of food to the Buddha and his five hundred attendants, a fine feast of fruit to be brought on platters. Then he told the servants who were to carry the fruit into the shrine room, "While you're still outside the shrine, spill the food on the ground."

So when they were bringing the food to the temple, they spilled it. Just as there are many beggars in India today, so there were then too, and the beggars came hurrying to take some food for themselves. The minister ordered the servants to beat the beggars back and, pointing out the old beggar woman, said, "Be especially rough on her." The servants began to beat and kick the old woman to keep her away from the food. She became so angry at this that she completely lost her sense of rejoicing in the king's merit: her rage utterly destroyed her positive attitude.

That day when the Buddha dedicated the merit at the meal, the king's name was back in the prayer.

Now there were many disciples present who were very disturbed at this and entertained a great deal of doubt; they could not understand why the Buddha had in the first place replaced the king's name with the old woman's, then later replaced the old woman's name with the king's. They asked the Buddha, and thus gave him an opportunity to explain that situations are not only shaped by the karmic process, but also demonstrate the extreme importance of our attitudes. In fact, our mental attitude is the most crucial factor in any situation.

6

Vows

For the practice of Dharma to be truly effective, two things are necessary. First, you must see that the essential nature of samsara is suffering and, on the basis of a thorough understanding of this suffering, desire to be liberated from unenlightened existence. Second, you must come to an appreciation of Enlightenment, or Buddhahood, and generate the desire to attain it. In this way, you make a choice between samsara, which you abandon, and Enlightenment, which you determine to achieve.

Although it may seem contradictory, in order to practice Dharma, we actually need to be just as concerned with the world as we are with Dharma practice—not in the sense of being caught up in worldly projects and schemes for making money, but in thinking about what it really means to live in this world. For example, we are human beings and subject, therefore, to the sufferings characteristic of our condition: birth, old age, sickness and death. We also belong to one of the six realms of samsaric existence, which encompass the experience of every being in this world. We must meditate again and again on the sufferings that attend each one of these states. This is the kind of concern with the world that is crucial for the practice of Dharma.

The Three Levels of Vows

Those who take ordination (dom pa [sdom pa]) as monks or nuns do so because they understand that involvement with the world is difficult and essentially fruitless. They take ordination to simplify their lives and direct themselves toward practice. Ordination is most important because it forms the vessel for our practice of Dharma. If we think of the Dharma as nectar, fine beer, or cream that is being poured into a bowl, then clearly, the vessel must be clean and without leaks. If not, whatever is poured into it will be spoiled or lost.

There are three levels of taking vows: the Hinayana or outer level; the Mahayana or inner level; and the Vajrayana or secret level. The ordination described above corresponds to what the Hinayana teachings call Pratimokśa, the vows of individual liberation, (so sor tar pay dom pa [so sor thar pa'i sdom pa]). It is the outer level of commitment to practice. The inner level corresponds to the contents of the vessel, which is the Bodhisattva vow in the Mahayana tradition. This is the development of compassion for all other beings and the deepening awareness of emptiness as the ultimate nature of all phenomena. The secret level is Vajrayana practice, like adding something to enrich the liquid in the vessel and make it even more delicious, as we might add milk, sugar, or salt to tea.

Many of us have taken a certain step in committing ourselves to the teachings, whether or not this is reflected in formal ordination. We may have vows of the layman, of the novice nun or monk, or of a fully ordained nun or monk. Many of us have taken the Bodhisattva vows, and all of us who are involved with the Vajrayana path have some commitment to the tantric vows, *samaya* [dam tshig].

We often fail to live up to vows we have taken, and when we fall short, Dorje Sempa meditation is very beneficial. It is also helpful to have a clear idea of just how difficult the vows may actually be to keep. Many people feel that a monk's vows or nun's vows, for example, are very difficult to keep, while the Bodhisattva vows are easy to keep and the Tantric vows involve no effort whatsoever, as if they kept themselves. Actually, the reverse is the case. If you are looking for vows that are easy to keep, the easiest by far are the monk's and nun's.

The famous Indian teacher Atiśa, who brought the teachings of the three *yanas* to Tibet, once said that when he undertook the practice of Buddhism, he first took the vows of a novice and then full ordination. By being scrupulously aware of the various rules of monastic conduct, he was able to preserve these vows without a single infraction. Later he went on to take the Bodhisattva vow only to find that he was breaking it quite regularly—several times a day he would catch himself in a particular thought or action contrary to its spirit. But he would not let an hour pass before he had recognized this, openly confessed it, and reconfirmed his dedication to the Bodhisattva vow.

Then after he had taken the tantric vows he compared the number of times he fell short to the particles of dust that would collect on a polished metal plate in a dust storm, or to the drops of rain in a downpour. His infractions were continual.

When people heard of Atiśa's report, they began worrying: "You seem to be saying, Lama, that once we have begun Vajrayana practice, there is no hope of achieving Enlightenment, because our vows will be continually broken."

Atiśa replied, "No, that's not the case at all. In fact, through the blessing of the Buddha we have skillful means to purify all our shortcomings, and many of our other negativities and unwholesome qualities as well." Then he taught the meditation of Dorje Sempa and its associated visualizations as an extremely effective way to purify not only infractions, but also our whole stream of being.

If we are aware of our body, speech, and mind as identical with the body, speech and mind of the Yidam, then all the tantric vows are included and fulfilled. When form is pure form, all sound is intrinsically mantra, and the mind is absorbed in the samadhi associated with the deity, then all vows are perfectly kept.

It is not the case that you must take ordination in order to be able to practice. You can develop compassion, meditate effectively, and realize Emptiness without any kind of formal commitment; but without that commitment you are far more likely to encounter many obstacles. With some commitment, such as ordination, or a disciplined way of life, there is a greater chance that your meditation will be effective, and that you will be able to carry it through to completion without many obstacles arising.

The Five Basic Commitments

Five vows are fundamental to all monks, nuns, and ordained laypersons. The first of these is the vow not to kill. If you have no such vow, it is more difficult to guard against the negative action of taking life. The act of killing creates a tremendous obstacle and contributes to hellish rebirth in future lives. Even in this life, we can see that people who kill others incur mental and physical suffering, loss of wealth, legal punishments, even the death penalty. So even on this obvious level, not taking life has benefits: peace of mind, avoidance of injury or the loss of wealth and freedom. If you are committed to the preservation of life, you avoid all these dangers.

The second vow is not to take what is not given. In one Tibetan word for thief, *kun ma* [rkun ma], the syllable 'ma' can mean "low" or "debased." It implies that stealing debases your own existence and makes you increasingly poor; it has a degenerative effect on your mind, wealth and enjoyment of life. The more you steal, the more you are deprived of what you are trying to get. In this life, there are penalties for theft: fines, jail sentences, and suffering. Furthermore, stealing contributes to states of deprivation and poverty in the future, and to rebirth as a hungry ghost. The vow not to steal helps you to avoid these unfavorable situations.

The third root vow is not to lie. Any lie you speak has a negative effect on your progress towards Enlightenment. It also gives you a reputation for never telling the truth. The one verbal action, however, that completely breaks the ordination is a lie regarding your attainment. You might present yourself as someone who has deep realization, when you have not, or give extensive and profound teachings as though you understood Dharma, when you do not. To confuse beings in this way is an extremely negative act, and the most serious kind of lie. In the Buddha's words, to commit this kind of lie is a greater negative action than to kill all the beings in the universe, because you cause beings to deviate from the Path of Liberation, lead them to lower states of existence, prolong the time they spend in samsara, and postpone their enlightenment. By lying about your attainment, you commit an action far worse than simply taking their lives. The third vow, therefore, commits us to avoid untruthful speech as much as possible and, especially, not to lie about our attainment.

In a monk's, nun's or celibate layperson's ordination, the fourth vow is to avoid all sexual activity. People are very attached to and concerned about sexual activity and take it to be a kind of bliss. Perhaps this is true on a relative level, but the ultimate state of bliss, of stable and permanent happiness, is incomparably beyond sexual experience; and, in a certain sense, sexual activity keeps you from this realization.

Vajrayana physiology describes the creative energy of the body as white *tig le* and red *tig le* [thig le] which are intimately connected with the experience of orgasm. If their potential is lost during sexual activity, this causes a state of discomfort or unease in body and mind that prevents us from achieving a stable state of bliss.

Celibacy is not abnormal repression or great hardship. On the contrary, it contributes to the achievement of true and stable happiness. The Buddha said that ordinary people take sexual enjoyment as the pinnacle of human happiness. But that kind of bliss only produces a certain sense of unease and discomfort in mind and body, because it can never be complete. This unfortunate state is like that of a old dog gnawing on a bone: the dog has no teeth to chew with and the hard bone actually cuts his gums; but he tastes the blood, and thinks, "Oh, this is delicious. I want to eat even more." So he continues chewing and chewing, not realizing that the delicious taste comes from his own blood. He gnaws the bone with bleeding gums and makes the wounds deeper and deeper; eventually, they become infected and turn into sores. What the dogs takes as ultimate happiness becomes pain.

In general, the problem with sexual attachment is perhaps not so much sexual activity in itself, but the fact that it leads to other things that are even more negative. For example, if a man and a woman are very attached to each other, and if the woman is attracted by another man, jealousy, anger, and obsession immediately arise in her lover's mind. As long as there is attachment, such emotions are present, like servants who follow a master. The point is that desire leads to many things that are far more negative and detrimental to your religious progress. The other problem, of course, is that when people have sexual relations they very often have children, and then find themselves completely involved in raising them, leaving much less time for Dharma practice. With the practical aims of simplifying your life, therefore, a celibate ordination is considered important for intensive practice.

In general, our emotions are such that the more we indulge them, the more we need to; the more we pay attention to them, the more inexhaustible they become. There is, however, a solution: we can simply cut off attachment and say, "Finished." We should approach the vow of celibacy with the attitude that sexual activity is no longer a part of our lives. There will be no difficulty as long as we have that total commitment. But as long as we pay attention to the emotions and indulge in them, they will continue to arise inexhaustibly.

After ordination, monks, nuns, and celibate laypersons should avoid any kind of frivolity — games, movies, television, dancing or singing. We may ask, "What's the harm in them? What's the benefit of giving them up?" First of all, they waste a good deal of time and promote various other activities which distract from practice. Secondly, they actually contribute to increasing the emotions. For example, while we are watching television, we are not practicing Dharma. Furthermore, what we see usually stimulates and encourages emotional responses, and thus works against the purpose of our ordination.

The fifth vow concerns the use of intoxicants, specifically alcohol, which obstructs the mental clarity that is so important in meditation, particularly for someone who is practicing the Vajrayana. In this tradition, it is said that if one is engaged in tantric practice, the loss of clarity through alcohol sows the seeds for rebirth in hell.

Alcohol is often referred to as the root of other problems. A traditional story tells of a pure and disciplined monk who went out one day to beg for food. He came to the door of a house where a woman invited him in for the noonday meal. Once she had him in the house, she locked the door and pointed to a goat standing in the corner of the main room and to a bottle of alcohol on the table. "You can either kill that goat, make love to me, or drink that alcohol," she said. "Unless you do one of the three, I won't let you out of this house." The monk thought to himself, "I'm an ordained monk. I can't make love to the woman. I can't kill an animal voluntarily, for I can't take life. I'm not supposed to drink, but it seems to be the least harmful of the actions." So saying, "I'll drink the alcohol," he downed the bottle. Becoming thoroughly intoxicated and consequently sexually aroused, he made love to the woman, became hungry, and killed the goat for food. In this way intoxication leads to many other things which can be more negative than the simple fact of intoxication itself.

Implicitly rejected in the fifth vow are also all kinds of drugs such as marijuana. The actual wording proscribes the use of fermented liquor, distilled liquor, and anything that intoxicates; it seems fairly obvious that something like marijuana intoxicates the mind. Some people think it produces a kind of bliss, and that may be true in an extremely brief and limited way, but basically it makes people stupid and lazy. They spend a lot of money for no purpose and get little done either in their worldly work or in Dharma practice. Eventually, they become very unhappy mentally and encounter many physical problems too. In short, marijuana robs the mind of clarity, causing it to wander and become distracted—a situation that is most detrimental to the development of effective meditation.

Tobacco, too, has a very detrimental effect on the body and mind. Padmasambhava, and many of the Nyingmapa *ter tons* [gter ston] who discovered his concealed teachings, were unanimous in saying that substances that are smoked contribute to lower states of rebirth—even when the smoke touches the body of someone not actually smoking. So if you have taken the vow to abandon intoxicants, you should avoid the use of alcohol, tobacco, marijuana, and all drugs that cloud the reason or otherwise impair the functioning of mind and body. For someone who doesn't have formal ordination, to avoid the use of intoxicants as much as possible is in itself a step forward. To be able to do without all these distractions, and concentrate our efforts on Dharma practice is a wonderful thing.

In the Buddha's teachings, we often find reference to the importance of moral discipline. "Morality is like the earth. It supports everything, animate and inanimate. It is the foundation of all positive qualities." Having moral discipline, another text says, we engage in study and contemplation of the teachings in order to enter into the effective practice of meditation. Some level of discipline is absolutely essential for our practice to be effective.

That doesn't mean that people who lack a high degree of discipline should feel discouraged or think, "I'm useless, I can't do anything. Without ordination I'm hopeless." That is not the point. Even for an ordinary person without formal ordination, the most important thing is to deal with life in as sensible a way as possible, so that we do not give rise to a great deal of anger, aggression, clinging, or greed. This is the crucial point.

For those who have taken ordination, another critical point is to guard against pride. Whether it is based upon your ordained status or on your erudition and intellectual understanding, pride goes against the purpose of practice and destroys its benefits. To think, "I'm a monk. I'm special, these people aren't. They're lower than I am," is an attitude completely contrary to the spirit of the ordination. It destroys the virtues you would otherwise develop by following the ordained way of life.

If you are quite intelligent, and your learning causes arrogance, you may think, "I'm superior to these simpletons. They don't understand as much as I do." Such intellectual pride runs contrary to a true understanding of Dharma, and, in fact, destroys much of the benefit of your practice. The Buddha compared pride to a hard rock on which drops of water can make no impression. These drops represent the positive qualities you develop through practice. If your pride has solidified to this extent, then there is no way for positive qualities to penetrate. Much the same thing happens if we regard Dharma simply as an intellectual pastime. If we merely accumulate information without practicing or experiencing what we have learned, our faith and compassion will diminish. We then become very indifferent to the teachings and think, "I've heard that before. I understand that already." If we persist in this callous attitude, we reach a state where we cannot be helped. We have cut ourselves off from all possibility of being rescued from our stupidity. The Buddha said that even the greatest evil-doer can be saved, but a person who has become apathetic towards the Dharma cannot be helped, because such a mind has become petrified and closed to the teachings. On the other hand, a Bodhisattva has gained a complete understanding of all aspects of Dharma as presented in the Sutras, the Vinaya (discipline), the Abhidharma, and so forth. In all descriptions of the Bodhisattva, however, there is never any reference to pride. Pride and realization are mutually exclusive.

When opportunities to practice Dharma occur, you should know that they arise from previous merit and that they afford a chance for you to accumulate further merit and develop awareness, and thus help other beings. You should also understand that it is because of the blessing of your Lama and the Three Jewels that you have such opportunities.

The focus of this teaching is to encourage people who are in a favorable situation, and not to discourage those who are not. There is no need to feel, "I'm only a layperson, just a householder (chim pa [khyim pa]). I haven't taken any vows, so I can't get enlightened. I'm hopeless." The point is to be encouraged to concentrate on what you do have, because at the very least you have the Seed of Buddhahood. You have the precious human birth, which provides the opportunity and the leisure to realize fully this inherent potential. You have met with the teachings of Dharma and, in particular, the teachings of the Vajrayana, which give you the means to realize the Enlightened Mind. Everything depends upon understanding what you have, recognizing the blessings of the situation, and then making diligent, intelligent use of them. This is the way to approach Enlightenment.

Is this to say that there is no difference between someone who holds ordination and someone who doesn't? No. There is a difference, which can be explained in the following way. Suppose there are two houses filled with identical treasure, exactly the same, except that one has a single door which is firmly bolted, and the other has many doors, all wide open. The house with the one door firmly bolted is in little danger of thieves, but the house with many open doors is always in danger of losing its precious contents. This is the difference between someone who has a formal discipline and lives up to it and someone who has not. Commitment to discipline through ordination gives the means to guard against faults and the loss of the benefits of Dharma practice. Without this formal commitment, one must have great diligence and intelligence, since the danger that mistakes will occur and benefits be lost is always present.

Questions and Answers

QUESTION: Some people are reluctant to take vows because they are afraid they may inadvertently break them, and then be in a worse situation than if they had never taken the vows. For example, a person might accidentally step on an insect.

ANSWER: Any act of killing breaks the vow, but the only act of killing that destroys the ordination is the willful murder of a human being. Even inadvertent killing would not break the vow completely. Aside from homicide, any other act of killing, intentional or not, is an infraction of the vow. In any case, killing is a negative act, whether or not you have taken the vow. You do not escape the consequences of even inadvertent killing and a certain element of bad karma is still involved. The purpose of the vow is to make a definite commitment to avoid killing.

Four considerations determine the gravity of any action. The four considerations are the object of the action, the intention, the act itself, and the completion of that act. In the case of killing, there is the person being killed, the intent to kill, the act of killing, and an actual death. These four elements must be present for the vow to be completely broken. If only three are present, the act is less serious. If there are only two or one, the repercussions diminish accordingly.

In the case of killing an insect, for example, there is initially the perception of the object, the thought "That is an insect, a living thing. It has consciousness." Second is the motivation. One thinks, "I want to kill it." The third stage is actually to kill it. And the fourth is that the insect dies and one thinks, "Ah, good, it's dead." That completes the action. This act of taking a life is serious because all four elements are present; that makes it a conscious act and fully carried out.

QUESTION: There are people who don't take vows but behave in accord with them, and other people who take the vows and keep them. Is there a difference?

ANSWER: There is a difference in the power of the virtue and merit accumulated by someone who is following a discipline without vows and someone who has actually taken formal ordination, because the latter has done so with a conscious intention and in the presence of their teacher and the Three Jewels. This adds an element of power to the situation that can be extremely effective. The difference is between natural virtue and deliberate virtue, which involves the conscious practice of a certain conduct. While the virtue of someone without ordination and someone with ordination, both living a good life, is more or less the same, what seems to be different is the degree of strength, real stability, and power to practice.

QUESTION: How can we develop discipline?

ANSWER: To develop a disciplined way of life, you need to look at your own situation. If you are a monk or a nun, a discipline is clearly defined, but for an ordinary person some examination is necessary. You need to look at the way you are living, and, when you realize that certain acts, killing for example, are negative, you no longer want to do them. At this point you are your own witness, and abstaining from a particular negative action like killing or stealing gives a great deal of benefit. If you do not feel you can be celibate, you can at least be faithful in your relationship, not deceiving or harming the other person. You make your own decisions and are your own witness for that kind of commitment. On the other hand, someone who has taken formal ordination has the best witnesses—the Three Jewels and the Lama; they make any action more powerful.

QUESTION: When I am taking a vow I get very nervous. I am afraid I will break it, and the presence of witnesses makes the whole thing even more unnerving.

ANSWER: It is not bad to feel nervous, because it means that you recognize you're undertaking something significant in the presence of an important witness. There is a sense of power and reality in the situation; it may frighten you, but it's not bad. It means you perhaps do not thoroughly understand the nature of what is going on, but at least you have some idea of the significance of the commitment. Still, if you feel that it would be detrimental at this time to undertake any formal commitment now, that does not mean that your own personal commitment isn't good enough. Human rebirth comes about as result of discipline, and discipline is not just a monk's or nun's vows: discipline is a certain commitment, whether by yourself or through formal ordination, to a way of life that pursues certain kinds of activity and avoids others. Perhaps in the present circumstances it would be better for you to avoid committing yourself to something that makes you nervous. Whether it is in the context of formal ordination or not, a vow is still effective and your own personal commitment to vows like not killing, lying or stealing, is important and very beneficial.

QUESTION: I have an extreme problem with discipline and an organized way of life. I'm afraid of the methods you describe, because I know they go against my own nature. On the other hand, I think I am sincerely open to the teaching. How can I keep on being open to the teaching, even when the idea of discipline is so distasteful?

ANSWER: That is the purpose of the Four Contemplations that Turn the Mind towards Dharma practice: they automatically give rise to commitment. Instead of trying to force the commitment, you simply meditate in such a way that commitment becomes the only choice open to you. Given the situation we are in, how else could we behave except to have this commitment? Having seen things clearly, commitment tends to develop by itself. Perhaps a story will illustrate this point.

During the lifetime of Buddha Shakyamuni, there was a young man who was one of the Buddha's cousins. His name was Chungawo [gCung dGa bo]. Chungawo was married to a very beautiful woman. They were extremely happy together, but overly attached to each other. They simply could not bear to be out of each other's presence: wherever they went and whatever they did, they were always together. One day the Buddha saw that his cousin was ripe for training, so he went on his begging rounds as usual, holding his bowl, and stood in the road before the gate of his cousin's house waiting to receive anything he might be offered.

Chungawo had great faith, and when he saw the Buddha standing there, he said to his wife, despite his extreme attachment to her, "I must go and make an offering to the Buddha."

As he was going out the door, his wife grabbed him and said, "Where are you going? Don't leave me." and he said, "No, I'm just going down to the end of the road. The Buddha's there. I'm going to offer him some food and I'll come right back." She reluctantly agreed, but taking part of the hem of her dress, she licked it and said, "I want you back before that's dry."

Chungawo said, "Yes," and went out to make his offering. When he had filled the Buddha's bowl, the Buddha handed it back to him and said, "Here, you carry this," and started walking away slowly down the path. Chungawo was torn for a moment because he longed to get back to his wife, but simply could not ignore the instruction of someone like the Buddha, so he began following him. The Buddha led him along a road up into the forest, to the place where he was staying, a small hermitage with a shrine. All along the road Chungawo could think of nothing but his wife, yet he was aware of his obligation to carry the Buddha's bowl, and at least hand it to him before he could run back home.

When they got to the hermitage the Buddha said, "Put the bowl down there. I'm leaving for a while, you stay here while I'm gone, and maybe sweep up a little. It's dusty, and there's a broom." Chungawo was in a quandary; a long time had already passed, it was getting later and later, and he wanted nothing more than to be back with his wife. But once again he felt some obligation to the Buddha, so he began to sweep as quickly as he could to get all the dirt out of the door so he could run down the road to his wife. But the more he swept the dirtier things seemed to get. As soon as he thought he had cleaned it all, he turned around and there was more dirt and dust on the floor than ever. So he started sweeping again, and again the dirt grew. This happened a number of times and finally he gave up, threw down the broom, and walked out of the hermitage.

There were two paths leading from the hermitage down to the village. One was the main broad path up which he had come with the Buddha and the other was an overgrown back path which wound down the hill. Chungawo thought, "I'll take the back path. I won't run into anybody and I'll get home as quickly as possible." But as he was going down this path, who should he see coming towards him but the Buddha. He thought, "I can't let him see me here," and ducked underneath a nearby bush. The branches of this bush hung down by the side of the road and formed a sort of little cave, into which Chungawo crawled, hoping to hide from the Buddha's gaze. But as the Buddha came up the path, the branches simply lifted up and there was Chungawo, crouching on the ground. The Buddha said, "What are you doing? Come with me." He took him back up the hill, and once again Chungawo found himself being led away from his wife and towards the hermitage.

This went on for days, as the Buddha continually found ways to keep him from returning home. Finally there came a point when Chungawo insisted that he simply couldn't stay any longer. So the Buddha said, "Well, all right, but just before you go, let me show you something. Take hold of my robe." Chungawo had no choice but to take hold of the Buddha's robes. All of a sudden he was flying through the air and then found himself on top of a high mountain, surveying a magnificent view in all directions.

While he and the Buddha were there enjoying the scenery, a very decrepit, wizened old woman approached them. The Buddha called Chungawo's attention to her and said, "Who is more beautiful, your wife or this old woman?" Chungawo exclaimed, "What do you mean? My wife is a hundred, no, a thousand times more beautiful than this old woman." The Buddha just said, "Let's go to the god realms. Take hold of my robes."

Chungawo did so, and immediately found himself in the god realms, a splendid environment of celestial palaces, with gods and goddesses enjoying sensual pastimes. Everything was so blissful that Chungawo was quite distracted from thoughts of his wife. Finally, after showing him the god realms, the Buddha took Chungawo to a palace inhabited by five hundred beautiful goddesses, where a central throne stood vacant. Then the Buddha said to Chungawo, "Who is more beautiful, your wife or these goddesses?" Chungawo said, "These goddesses are a thousand times more beautiful than my wife." And the Buddha said, "Find out what's going on here." Chungawo approached one of the goddesses, and said, "Why is there no one on the central throne?" She replied, "There's no one to occupy it just yet. A human named Chungawo is thinking about taking ordination. He will become a monk and practice Dharma very strenuously. The virtue he accumulates will earn him a rebirth in this god realm. This is the seat he will occupy."

Chungawo went back to the Buddha as quickly as he could and said, "Could I take ordination now?" The Buddha said, "That would be fine." They returned to the human realm and the Buddha bestowed the vows of a fully ordained monk upon Chungawo, who became a member of the Buddhist community and began practicing diligently.

One day the Buddha called all his monks together and said, "All my disciples are very good monks. You are all dedicated to attaining complete Enlightenment for the benefit of all beings. Except one, Chungawo—the only reason he keeps his vows is to gain rebirth in the god realms, where he wants to enjoy worldly pleasure. You should have nothing to do with him. I don't want you to talk to him, or share a seat with him. Ignore him completely."

Now Chungawo was doing his best to be a very pure, disciplined monk, a good disciple of the Buddha. His memory of the goddesses had made him forget all about his wife, and he was busy trying to keep his vows as well as he could. Suddenly he discovered he was being ostracized. Nobody would speak to him. As soon as he spoke, people turned their backs and walked away. They would neither sit with him nor eat with him, and he became extremely depressed. Finally, he went to the Buddha and said, "What's wrong with me? Why does everyone ignore me?"

The Buddha said, "Don't worry, let's go visit the hell realms this time. Take hold of my robe." Chungawo did so and they soon arrived. The Buddha took him through one of the hells, where they saw beings burned, boiled, sawn in half or undergoing other tortures as a result of previous karma, and then they came to a vast pot full of molten metal. Fiendish-looking beings were stirring the pot, although no one was actually in it. So Chungawo went up to one of them and said, "Why are there beings in all the other pots, but this one is empty?" And the fiend said, "There is a monk named Chungawo, who thinks he is keeping his displine very purely. That merit will earn him rebirth in the god realms, but once that's exhausted, this is going to be his home." Chungawo became extremely frightened and the Buddha took him back to the human realm.

At that point, Chungawo realized that any concern with the world was pointless, and that he should really be completely focused on attaining enlightenment. He became a very accomplished meditator who was noted for his ability to absorb himself completely in meditation, to rest his mind one-pointedly without any sensory distraction.

The point of the story is that by understanding death and impermanence, the sufferings of samsara and the karmic process, you spontaneously discover a commitment to pure Dharma practice.

Ordination, which helps to cut off certain activities that are harmful to oneself and others, is one way of dealing with the emotions, and a very effective one. But not everyone has to take ordination; indeed, it is very difficult for most people to undertake something as drastic as monastic ordination, where one leaves one's family and so forth, and becomes a monk or a nun. It is not possible or practical for most people, and they should not feel that ordination is absolutely necessary: there are other ways of dealing with the emotions. Thanks to the kindness and blessings of the Buddha, we have instructions regarding Bodhicitta, the love and compassion for all other beings. There are also ways of skillfully transmuting the emotions without having to cut them off or suppress them. So one does not have to sever connections with family and friends.

The last words the Buddha spoke before he passed into Nirvana were: "I have shown you the way to Liberation. Actually achieving it is up to you." The teacher can show the way to Liberation, but we have to experience it for ourselves. The path of Bodhicitta is open to all of us.

QUESTION: How is the merit of virtuous action lost?
ANSWER: The causes of losing merit and the benefits of our practice fall into three principal categories. The first is pride in what we have accomplished. It is detrimental to think, "I'm a wonderful person to have been so virtuous and accumulated this merit. I must be quite special." A second way of impairing the effectiveness of merit involves regret, for example, following an act of generosity with the thought, "Oh, I shouldn't have given all that away, that was stupid." The third way is through anger. Giving rise to very strong malevolent emotions destroys or impairs the merit of virtuous practice. We guard against this loss by sharing the merit. As long as merit remains our own, it may be destroyed, but once we have

sincerely and without attachment shared it with everyone, it cannot be impaired even in these three ways. Through the simple act of sharing we guard against all these negative emotions.

7

Women, Siddhi, *Dharma*

Women and men, children and adults, all share, to some extent, the opportunities and freedoms of our human condition (see Glossary, "Precious Human Birth"). By contrast, animals and those in other states of existence lack these opportunities and freedoms. The distinction between human and beast—wild carnivores living in the jungles, deep sea creatures or insect life—is made precisely on the basis of this opportunity to practice the Dharma.

Even among human births, there is a tremendous variety in our capacities to recognize and use this opportunity. The most excellent kind of human birth is called *precious*; in it, a person can make meaningful use of his or her life. This has nothing to do with social standing or any of the ordinary ways in which we judge people; it certainly makes no difference, for example, whether one is a woman or man: the only question is whether or not the advantages of a human rebirth are appreciated and employed.

Regardless of whether you are a man or a woman, regardless of your particular situation in this life, if you have faith, confidence, and diligence, if you have compassion and wisdom, you can become enlightened. If you are merely caught up in your emotional confusion and continue to let that dominate your life, no matter whether you are a man or a woman, Enlightenment will be difficult to attain. But if you have the necessary qualities for Dharma practice, the kind of body you have makes no difference at all.

The Ultimate Nature of Mind is Neither Male nor Female

The reason for this total equality of opportunity is the nature of mind itself, which is neither male nor female. There is no such thing as the intrinsic nature of one person's mind being better than someone else's; on the ultimate level the empty, clear and unimpeded nature of mind exhibits no limiting qualities such as maleness or femaleness, superiority or inferiority. On the worldly level, of course, there are situations in which one person's mind suffers more obscurations than another's. This has more to do with karma than with gender or social standing. Even in the various realms of rebirth, there is no ultimate difference between one mind and another. The profound teachings of the Buddhadharma provide ways to eliminate obscurations and arrive at a direct experience of mind.

On a relative level, however, there are differences, including the way in which the physical embodiment is formed at the subtle level of energy channels and energy centers. According to the teachings of tantra, the way in which a mind incarnates in a male body is subtly different from the way in which it incarnates in a female body. In the psycho-physical make-up of a male, there is more force, more concentrated and direct energy, whereas in that of a female there is more spaciousness, signifying Wisdom. These relative differences should always be understood in the context of the ultimate nature of mind.

If in studying and practicing the Buddha's teachings, women understand what is being said, they will attain Enlightenment. If men understand, they will attain Enlightenment.

In the Vajrayana tradition, the lives of the Mahasiddhas of Buddhist India represent models of Dharma practice. Among these are men such as Tilopa and Naropa and women such as Sukasiddhi and Niguma whose Enlightenment came about because they made the fullest possible use of a human birth, not because they were in a particular kind of body.

Tara, the Protector

One great Bodhisattva, however, is always associated with the female form. This is Tara, the Liberator. Of her origin, this story is told.

Many millions of years in the past, there was a certain universe in which lived a princess, a young woman who was the daughter of the king of the realm. Her name was Yeshe Dawa [ye shes zla ba], which means "Moon of Primordial Awareness." And at that time in that world there was a Buddha whose name was Tönyö Drupa [don yod grub pa]. The princess developed a great faith in this Buddha and received teachings from him. In particular she received instructions in generating Bodhicitta, the compassionate concern for all other beings. The special vow the princess made was that until she achieved Enlightenment she would continue to incarnate as a woman, always taking a female form to benefit beings through her Buddha activity. Having made this initial vow, through her Bodhicitta, she donned the armor of this commitment. Overcoming all obstacles, she worked courageously to accumulate merit, to deepen her awareness, and to make herself more effective in helping sentient beings liberate themselves from confusion.

When teaching the root tantra associated with Tara, the Buddha praised this great Bodhisattva: "Tara is she who frees and protects beings from all possible fears and sufferings that they can encounter. Tara is she who closes the doors to the lower realms of existence. Tara is she who leads them on the path to higher states of being." With these words, the Buddha extolled the virtue of Tara in granting us protection and deliverance from all the fears that are part of the human condition.

Another way of conceiving of Tara is as an emanation of Chenrezi, the Bodhisattva of Compassion. At one time, Chenrezi, viewing the suffering of all beings throughout the world, was so moved that he shed two tears; the tear that fell from his right eye turned into the green form of the Bodhisattva Tara, and the tear from the left eye became the white form.

Machik Drupay Gyalmo and Tipupa

Amitayus is the Buddha of Immortality. One great Siddha noted for her practice of Amitayus was a woman called Machik Drupay Gyalmo [ma gcig grub pa'i rgyal mo]. She meditated upon this deity and attained not only Enlightenment, the ultimate goal of such practice, but also the more mundane accomplishment of prolonging her life. Tradition has it that she lived five hundred years through her practice of Amitayus.

While Machik Drupay Gyalmo was still alive and teaching in India, there flourished another celebrated teacher, Tipupa. His interesting history goes back to southern Tibet in the area of Lodrak where Marpa the Translator lived. Marpa had a number of sons; to the eldest, Tarma Doday [dar ma mdo sde], Marpa intended to pass on his transmission. Marpa was thwarted by the untimely death of Tarma Doday, who was thrown from his horse and suffered a fatal concussion. Before the young man died, however, he was able to make use of a technique his father had taught him: he was able to transfer his consciousness, not from the physical body to a state of enlightened awareness, but into another physical body, a corpse. The practice required that the body, whether human or not, have only recently died and be fit to receive life. The mind of the dying person could then be projected into that corpse and reanimate it to carry on life as before.

The problem, of course, is that a new corpse is not always easy to find. When Marpa's son died, the whole area was searched and all that could be found was a dead pigeon. Someone had seen it struck by a hawk in the air and knocked out of the sky; it was dead when it fell to the ground. So he picked up the warm corpse of the pigeon and went running back to Marpa. They placed the pigeon on Tarma Doday's breast, and as his body began to die, the pigeon came to life, shaking its feathers and sitting up.

Marpa kept the pigeon for several days, feeding it well, and taking good care of it. While he was meditating, he realized what needed to be done. Marpa told his son, now incarnate as the pigeon,

about a charnel ground in India. Having been there himself, Marpa
knew the directions and outlined the way very clearly. Marpa lived
near the southern border of Tibet, where the journey to India is
relatively short through the low passes over the Himalayas. "Fly to
India," he said, "and find this charnel ground. The cremation of a
young man is about to take place. You will be able to transfer your
consciousness from the pigeon's body to his, and thus experience
human existence again." Then he let the pigeon go. It circled three
times around Marpa and his wife, and flew off south.

When the bird reached India, it found the funeral procession,
led by a Brahmin couple whose fifteen-yer-old son, bright and full
of promise, had contracted an infectious disease and suddenly died.
As the mourners laid the corpse out for cremation, the pigeon landed on the head, and immediately fell over dead. Right then the boy
began to wake and move again. At first the onlookers thought a
ghoul had taken possession of the corpse and ran away in fright. But
the boy was able to speak to them, and soon convinced the brahmin
family that their son had indeed come back to life, and without the
help of demons.

In time this boy grew up to become a famous Buddhist
meditator and teacher. Because of the pigeon that landed on his
corpse, people called him Tipupa, meaning "Pigeon Boy," but his
personal name was Trimay Shenyen [dri med bshes gnyen] which
means "undefiled spiritual friend."

Tipupa was still alive and teaching in India when Milarepa's
student Rechungpa [ras chung pa] decided to go there to seek out
teachings the lineage had not yet received. He met and studied with
Tipupa, and one day was going through a bazaar when someone approached him out of nowhere and said, "Well, if it isn't the young
Tibetan yogin. You're in a lot of trouble. You have only seven days
to live. Such a pity!" and then disappeared. Rechungpa was
shocked, and wondered if the omen was genuine. He hurried to his
teacher, Tipupa, who said, "It appears that this was an accurate
prediction. A big obstacle to your life is coming, and unless you can
deal with it skillfully, you will die. The most effective thing I can
recommend is for you to go to see the woman teacher who is very
skillful at transmitting the practice of Amitayus, the practice of immortality and longevity."

The woman was Machik Drupay Gyalmo. She was called Machik, "one mother" or "only mother," since she was maternally affectionate towards her students, who came to regard her as a mother. Drupay Gyalmo means "Queen of Siddhas." Tipupa sent Rechungpa to take teachings from her; by receiving the Amitayus empowerment and practice, Rechungpa was able to forestall the threat to his life. Through his connection with Machik, he received the teachings he would bring back to Tibet, where they entered into all the lineages of Tibetan Buddhism, especially the mainstream of the Kagyü school. To this day we find reference to the Longevity Empowerment of the Queen of Siddhas.

Gelongma Palmo

During the early development of Buddhism in India, before its transmission to other countries like Tibet, there lived a princess, daughter of an Indian king, an unusually beautiful and intelligent girl, a most promising heir to the kingdom. At a certain point in her youth, however, she contracted a particularly virulent form of a disease resembling leprosy. Open sores began to cover her entire body and her flesh started to fester. As terrible as this was, doctors could find no cure. Gradually it became obvious that she was becoming a dangerous source of contagion and, as the disease progressed, she became disgusting to see. So cutting off all ties with her life as a princess, she left the palace and went into a forest hermitage. She took the vows of a nun in order to devote the last years of her life to intense Dharma practice.

During this time, she met a teacher who became very fond of her and was deeply moved by her situation. This teacher gave her the empowerment and the instruction for meditation on the eleven-faced, thousand-armed form of Chenrezi. For several years this was her main practice. During this time her disease got worse and worse; her extremities began to rot away, and her whole body was so completely covered with open sores that she couldn't even sleep at night; she was in extreme pain and dying. Then, in the semi-waking state that was her fitful way of sleeping, she had a dream, or vision: the impression that somebody dressed in brilliant white came into her room with a large vase filled with pure water and poured it all over her body. She felt that the disease was being shed like the skin of a snake, and that her body was being made whole again. When she woke up, she found her body renewed, as though nothing had ever troubled it. There was no sign of disease. Instantly she was filled with intense devotion and the conviction that her cure was due to the blessings of Chenrezi. At that moment she began to pray and meditate, and was blessed with a direct vision of the Bodhisattva, who dissolved into her. With this experience she attained a very high state of Realization and the direct experience of the nature of her mind.

The nun's name was Palmo [dpal mo], which means Lady of Glory, and she is known to the tradition as Gelongma Palmo. "Gelongma" [dge slong ma] simply means a fully ordained Buddhist nun. The teachings connected with the fasting ritual of the thousand-armed, eleven-faced form of Chenrezi were principally developed and spread by this nun; in fact, this popular practice is still referred to as the method or tradition of Gelongma Palmo. Many people used it as one of their main practices and now that Tibetan Lamas are bringing this meditation to the West, many westerners have also been inspired by it, and have taken part in *nyung nay* [smyung gnas], the fasting ritual.

Niguma, Chungpo Naljor, and Sukhasiddhi*

Because of the great wisdom, learning and skillfulness the Buddha embodies, he gave appropriate teachings to counteract all our emotional afflictions — eighty-four thousand different ones are mentioned. To eliminate them, he gave eighty-four thousand teachings, traditionally known as the Eighty-four Thousand Collections. Twenty-one thousand emotional afflictions arise from the root poison of desire. As an antidote for these, the Buddha explained the teachings of the Vinaya collection, the prescriptions for ethical behavior. To eliminate the twenty-one thousand emotional afflictions arising from hatred, he gave the twenty-one thousand teachings that make up the Sutra collection. The twenty-one thou-

---

*At this point the text follows a teaching by Lama Norlha on three teachers fundamentally important to the Shangba Lineage and, through it, to other traditions of practice in Tibet.

sand teachings given in the Abhidharma, the third collection, were designed to annihilate the twenty-one thousand emotional afflictions arising from the root of ignorance. Yet there remain twenty-one thousand which result from the complex intermixture of the three—desire, hatred and ignorance. As antidotes to these, the Buddha gave the twenty-one thousand teachings which make up tantra, the teachings of the Vajrayana.

The teachings given by the Buddhas are not intellectual speculation, but are based on their personal experience of absolute Enlightenment. Having given up all that concerns "me" and "I," and having committed themselves to the benefit of all beings, whatever the difficulties, Buddhas continually experience perfect Enlightenment. These enlightened beings manifest in skillful ways to liberate beings, using whatever forms or appearances are appropriate.

Thus Buddhas and Bodhisattvas take all sorts of births: sometimes they come as kings and queens, princes, ministers, sometimes as commoners, peasants, animals—whatever is most practical to benefit beings, whatever is necessary to present the Dharma. Sometimes they appear as men. Sometimes as women. I will tell the story of two women, Niguma and Sukhasiddhi, who took the responsibility of demonstrating the Dharma in such a way that their teachings continue to benefit sentient beings to this day.

Niguma

Niguma was born in Kashmir, a Muslim country, in a region called the Land of Great Magic. During the time of the previous Buddha, this land had been covered by water, and a naga king was in possession of it. An arhat, who was a disciple of the Buddha of that time, longed to erect a temple there, so he went to ask the naga king for a piece of solid ground. The naga king promised one, but only as big as the arhat's body could cover when he was sitting in meditation. The arhat gratefully accepted what was offered, and when the time came to take possession of the land, he performed a miracle: his sitting body covered the whole of that land. The naga king kept his promise, and the whole new land was offered to the arhat, whose name was Nyimay Gung.

With his miraculous power, the arhat made all the water disappear, and a magnificent temple and monastery were soon built there. People in the surrounding regions began to take notice of this new landscape and, especially, its most beautiful temple. They wanted to live there and discussed how to go about it. They finally decided to invite a great magician who could create a city all round the temple. Once he had done this and before he could undo his magical creation (as magicians are wont to do), the people destroyed him. So the settlement continued there, and the district acquired the reputation of a land of great magnificence and great magic.

This special place later became the birthplace of many mahasiddhas, among them Naropa. And here too was born the great female Bodhisattva Niguma, who by auspicious coincidence happened to be born as the sister of Naropa, in a virtuous, noble family. In former lives she had generated the enlightened mind and followed the path of the Bodhisattvas. She now chose voluntary birth as a woman who would benefit and liberate others. During her lifetime as Niguma, the experiences and profound teachings that she had made her own in many previous eons were now further enlarged and reviewed with the other learned Mahasiddhas of her time. As Niguma, she experienced the perfect state of the ultimate awakened mind. Enlightenment manifested through her so that her entire being, including her physical form, transcended mundane existence, and experienced perfect Buddhahood within her lifetime.

Niguma received the ultimate teachings directly from Vajradhara, the primordial Buddha, in the form of personal initiation into all levels of the teachings—Sutra, Abhidharma, and Tantra. As a result, she manifested as a tenth stage Bodhisattva; this means that even the subtlest obscurations were dispelled, so that her mind became one with the mind of the Buddha, attaining the Three Bodies of perfect Enlightenment. From her lifetime to this present day, she continues to manifest whatever subtle or more material form is necessary to benefit beings over limitless time.

Her foremost disciple was the Mahasiddha Chungpo Naljor [khyung po rnal 'byor], who was born in Tibet and travelled to India to receive the full transmission from her. In granting him the empowerments, Niguma also confirmed that not only he, but all his successors and followers would in the future have the good fortune to receive the blessing of dakinis, encounter enlightened beings, and perfect Liberation.

Chungpo Naljor

Chungpo Naljor was born in a year of the tiger in the southern part of Tibet, into a distinguished family. Chungpo is the family name—the clan of the *khyung*, or Garuda, the legendary great bird that is guardian of the north. His father's name was Chungpo Chujar, and his mother's, Tashi. Thus, his own name meant "the yogin of the Garuda clan."

A portent marked his birth: The great Mahasiddha Amogha came flying through the air from India and made the prophecy that this newborn child, who was already highly realized, would in time come to India and there receive the profound transmissions that would make him a greater guide of beings.

The qualities of Chungpo Naljor began to manifest while he was still very young. When he was five years old, he told detailed stories about his past existences, and revealed insight into his lives to come, and into the future in general. By the age of ten, he had completed the secular curriculum, the studies any learned person would undertake: philosophy, astrology, astronomy, and so on. By his twelfth year he had commenced the study of religion, beginning with Bon. He then began studying and practicing Nyingma teachings, including the core practice of Dzok chen [rdzogs chen], the Great Perfection.

At this point Chungpo Naljor journeyed to India, where he studied with many learned and highly realized beings. Foremost among them were the two dakinis, Sukhasiddhi and Niguma. From them he received the ultimate pith instructions which led him to experience the highest stages of the Bodhisattva's path and established his mind in the enlightened state of Dorje Chang.

His meeting with Niguma came about in this fashion. After he had received teachings from many great Siddhas, Chungpo Naljor again searched for highly realized teachers from whom he could receive more advanced instruction. The most realized teachers he encountered told him that one with his qualities should seek the great Bodhisattva who was not separate from Dorje Chang in her realization and in the profound teachings she could skillfully transmit.

Chungpo Naljor asked where he could meet such an enlightened being and was told that her presence could manifest anywhere to highly purified beings. Unfortunate beings, those still caught in emotional afflictions, would find it very difficult to encounter her at all, since she had dissolved her physical form, attained the rainbow body, and achieved the level of Dorje Chang. Every now and again, however, she would visit the most sacred cremation grounds and, leading a host of dakinis, would preside over great ritual offering feasts, *ganacakras* (tso chi kor lo [tshogs kyi 'khor lo]). There someone might have an opportunity of seeing the great Niguma.

As soon as Chungpo Naljor heard the name of the great dakini, he felt such devotion, like an electric shock, that tears welled up in his eyes. Immediately he set out to find her at the great charnel ground called Sosaling [so sa gling]. As he travelled, he continuously made supplications to the Three Jewels. When he reached the cemetery, he saw above him in space at the height of seven banana trees, a female deity bluish in appearance, who wore elaborate bone ornaments and held a trident and a skull. As he gazed at her, he sometimes saw one deity, and sometimes many; some were in meditation posture, and some were dancing or making graceful gestures. He felt sure that this was the great Bodhisattva Niguma, and began to make reverent prostrations to her, sincerely imploring her for transmission of the teachings.

Niguma mocked his request and sneering, warned him, "I am a flesh-eating dakini and I have a large retinue of other dakinis like myself. When they come, we may eat you. Run away before it's too late!"

But her words did not dismay Chungpo Naljor or make him retreat. Again he proclaimed his longing to receive the transmission from her. After his second plea, Niguma made this stipulation: he must offer gold if he really wished to receive teachings from her. Fortunately, Chungpo Naljor had five hundred gold pieces with him, and these he took out and tossed up to her as an offering. As the gold came into her hands, she scattered it into the air, so that it fell all over the forest. This behavior just increased Chungpo

Naljor's confidence that she was indeed the great Niguma. A flesh-eating dakini would certainly have felt attachment to the gold and kept some.

With deepening conviction he continued to beseech her for the teachings; Niguma turned her head from side to side, and looked into the different directions with her blazing eyes. So summoned, a great throng of dakinis surrounded her, all busily at work. Some were building palaces, some constructing mandalas, and others were making preparations for Dharma teaching, and for the *ganacakra* that would follow.

On the day of the full moon, Niguma gave Chungpo Naljor the empowerment and transmission of the teachings of the profound Dream Practice. In the middle of this, she said to him: "Son from Tibet, arise!"

Suddenly Chungpo Naljor found himself in midair at the height of three banana trees. Looking up towards Niguma, he saw that the great being was on top of a golden mountain, surrounded by a vast retinue of dakinis. Down the four sides of the mountain, rivers fell. Chungpo Naljor wondered out loud if this amazing mountain was truly there or whether he was witnessing a miraculous performance by the dakini.

Niguma answered, "When the ocean of samsara is turned over, when all attachment and ego-clinging are totally uprooted, then every place and every thing is covered with gold, forming a golden field of non-attachment. The actual nature of samsara, this phenomenal world, is like a play of dreams and illusion. When you have realized experientially that the play of the phenomenal world is nothing but a dream, or is like the illusion created by some magician, then you have gone beyond the ocean of samsara. This requires the greatest devotion to your Lama. Understand this. Now you must leave here. Go and grasp your dream!"

Chungpo Naljor understood her instructions and entered the dream as he had been taught. In the dream state he was given full empowerment for the Five Golden Dharmas of Niguma. Three times in the dream he received the empowerments, including those of the Six Yogas of Niguma. At the end, Niguma told him this: "In this land there have been no other beings except yourself who received the total transmission of these doctrines three times in one dream."

On the following day, Niguma once again gave him three times the complete transmissions, with the detailed explanations of these doctrines; this time the transmission took place in the waking state. One commitment she asked him to keep was this: only he and another Mahasiddha, by the name of Lavapa, had had the transmission into the six doctrines of Niguma; the teachings should be kept secret until seven generations had passed in an unbroken line of transmission from one Lama to one chosen disciple in each generation. After the seventh generation, it would be appropriate to give these teachings more widely for the benefit of all beings. Niguma's prayers of aspiration and her blessing would be directed toward that end.

There is really no essential difference between the Six Yogas of Naropa and the Six Doctrines of Niguma. The notable difference is in the transmission lineage. The Six Doctrines of Naropa came from Naropa to Marpa and his successors, while the Six Doctrines of Niguma came through the great Mahasiddha Chungpo Naljor. Thereafter, the two doctrines were transmitted by the successive lineage holders so that there is to the present day an unbroken line in the Kagyü tradition of both doctrines, Naropa's and Niguma's.

Sukhasiddhi

At another point in his career Chungpo Naljor questioned the Mahasiddha Aryadeva about those who would be able to advance his understanding. Aryadeva said that he himself had received teachings for seven months from a highly realized dakini, whose instructions had brought him to the eighth Bodhisattva level. Then, urging Chungpo Naljor to search her out for himself, he told the story of how the dakini, whose name was Sukhasiddhi, had herself achieved realization.

In that same area of India where Niguma had lived, there was a great city in which lived a family: a father, mother, three sons, and three daughters. A time came when that land suffered such a terrible famine that this family's provisions were reduced to one small jar of rice, which they were keeping as a last resource. In desperation, the three sons left home and went towards the north, the three daughters towards the west, and the father towards the south, all searching for food, but all in vain. While they were away on their futile search, the mother stayed at home. One day there came to her door a great Siddha, who by his clairvoyance knew that she had a jar of rice tucked away. He told the mother that he had not eaten for a very long time, and begged her to offer him some of the rice. Moved by his plea and by his virtue, she offered him the rice, cooking it for him and eating a little herself. When the sons, daughters and father came back empty-handed, exhausted and famished, they told the mother to bring out the last of the rice, so they could have at least one meal. Then she had to confess that there was no rice, that she had given it to a Siddha who had come begging. She explained that she had been certain that at least one of them would bring some food home, so she had felt it proper to offer the rice.

They were all outraged and turned her out of the house; she would have to go her own way and take care of herself.

She had never been away from her family before. She went among her neighbors asking for advice. Everywhere she got the same suggestion: she should go to the west, to Oddiyana, a rich country whose people were understanding and generous. There she might find the basic necessities of life.

So the mother went to Oddiyana and found that its people were indeed sympathetic. She had come at an auspicious time, the season of the harvest, and the people gave her quantities of rice. She took that rice to a town called Bita and used it to make *chang*, a kind of beer. She sold the *chang*, bought rice with the proceeds, made more *chang*, and so gradually began to make her living as a brewer. She was soon able to open an inn, and amongst the people who came to buy her wares was one regular customer, a young girl who came every day to buy *chang* and meat. The mother became curious about this girl, who never ate or drank anything, but carried it all away. Where was she taking it? One day she ventured to ask the girl. The young woman answered, "Quite a way from here in the mountains, there is a great Mahasiddha, Virupa, who is constantly in meditation. Every day I take this as an offering to him."

The mother thought about this, and said, "In that case, I would certainly like to make my *chang* an offering to the great Mahasiddha."

She went on to tell the young woman the story of her misfortunes, her exile from her family, and how now in her declining years she was realizing the futility of involvement with material existence. As a way of accumulating merit, she wanted to make offerings of her *chang* to the Mahasiddha.

From that time forward, she regularly offered the best *chang* to the Mahasiddha, and the young attendant brought it every day to the master. One day Virupa happened to ask how she was able to bring *chang* and meat every day without ever having to pay anything — who was making these offerings? The young woman explained that an elderly woman, new to the town, seemed very devoted to him and wanted to make regular offerings.

The great master Virupa said, "Today this elderly woman, who must already be someone of great merit, should be brought to me in person. I will guide her to complete Liberation." When this message was brought by Virupa's young attendant, the mother grew excited, and taking along generous offerings of *chang* and meat, went to visit Virupa.

When she came into his presence, Virupa bestowed Empowerment upon her. She was ripe for such an experience and in many ways was nearly a realized yogini already. The transmissions Virupa gave enhanced her Realization, with the result that she became a great Dakini. This woman, who was to be called Sukhasiddhi, was fifty-nine years old when she was banished from her family, and it had taken her a year to establish a livelihood, so when she received the profound instructions from Virupa she was sixty-one. With one-pointed conviction and commitment she received the totality of the empowerment and became an enlightened Dakini not only in essence, but also in form and appearance. She took on the form of a sixteen year old maiden.

Sukhasiddhi was completely dedicated to practice and had surrendered her ties to the phenomenal world. Through practice and devotion she in time equalled in Realization other great yoginis such as Niguma. Like them, she had visions of Dorje Chang from whom she received complete transmissions. After attaining such Realization, she devoted her profound abilities to manifesting in ways that would help and guide other beings. For over a thousand years since then fortunate beings have been and still are able to perceive Sukhasiddhi, in the form of an unchanging, youthful woman.

This was the story Aryadeva told Chungpo Naljor about the life and Liberation of Sukhasiddhi. Aryadeva went on to explain that sometimes on the tenth day of the month, Sukhasiddhi could be seen in the thick of a certain forest, surrounded by a retinue of Dakinis. Fortunate beings sometimes encountered her there, if she made herself visible to them.

So Chungpo Naljor, carrying gold to offer, went towards the forest as he had been directed. There, above a most beautiful juniper tree, a great Dakini was to be seen, brilliantly white, her hand in the "unborn" mudra. She was surrounded by a retinue of other Dakinis in the midst of a vast cloud of light. At his first sight of this great being, intense devotion was born in the heart of Chungpo Naljor; his hair stood on end, and tears sprang to his eyes. The presence of the Dakini brought immense joy like that at the attainment of the first Bodhisattva level.

He made offerings of flowers, and circumambulated the tree below the great Dakini and her retinue. With a one-pointed mind, he begged her to teach. Sukhasiddhi said that the teachings she held were the highest in the Vajrayana, transmitted to her directly by Dorje Chang; to be worthy of receiving them, he must have an accumulation of merit, and make offerings of precious substances such as gold. Then, with palms joined together, he must generate intense devotion in order to receive the Empowerment, the Scriptural Transmission and the Instruction (*wang, lung* and *tri*, the three phases of preparation in the Vajrayana). Chungpo Naljor was directed to sit in the most respectful position to receive the profound teachings. Looking at him, Sukhasiddhi said that the experience of the precious human birth, and the opportunity of receiving the supreme Dharma in her presence was a great wonder.

In this way Chungpo Naljor made offerings and received her instruction. Sukhasiddhi told him that in the future he would be the main lineage-holder of the teaching she had transmitted, and that the teaching itself would continue to exist and be available for the benefit of beings. Chungpo Naljor received the four empowerments — of body, speech, mind, and the union of all three — into the Six Doctrines of Sukhasiddhi, which are similar to the Six Doctrines of Niguma. Then she prophesized that he would attain supreme Enlightenment and from the pure realm of Amitabha his activities would benefit all. Sukhasiddhi's Realization as embodied in her teachings has continued to this present day through practitioners in many countries of the world.

Deeds of Bodhisattvas Awaken Confidence

Stories about the lives of enlightened beings provide us with examples of conduct that will inspire us and, especially, arouse a confidence that we too can follow in their footsteps. Our commitment to Dharma and our practice of it can result in exactly the same sort of Enlightenment we see manifested in their lives. A strong sense of conviction and of dedication is essential, as we can see in the life of the great yogi Milarepa. After all the exhausting tasks Marpa had set him were completed, Milarepa was finally able to see the manifestation of Marpa as the Yidam Hevajra — in form as well as essence. After Marpa had appeared with all the splendors and ornaments of the Yidam, he asked what Milarepa had experienced. Milarepa said that devotion had arisen in him, and confidence that such a state as Marpa had manifested could be realized. Milarepa then made a one-pointed aspiration to achieve it himself.

In our own situation as intelligent beings able to communicate, listen, make sense and explain, we have to understand clearly the distinction between samsara and Nirvana, learn what really needs to be done, and then take practical steps to do it. That is the real teaching and intention of the Buddha.

The greater our involvement in samsara, the greater our suffering. That is how things work. The Buddha said, "The greater the power, the greater the misery; the greater the wealth, the greater the miserliness; the more caught up we are in samsaric situations, the greater our self-deception." We have to realize that what we want to experience, and can experience, is ultimate happiness, a state that is indestructible, beyond circumstances and conditioning factors. To attain this we must give up temporary satisfactions, which in any case are full of false promises and pretense. We go to restaurants and social spots to have fun, to try to cheer one another up and grasp some measure of good feeling and security. Even if we don't mean it, we say how good everything looks, how well everything is going, and so on. But eventually we have to face reality, and that's very painful. The more we try to run away from suffering by pretending that it really doesn't exist, the more suffering we bring ourselves. That is not the way of Dharma. If you have recognized your need for Enlightenment, you will give up these deceptive pursuits and work towards ultimate happiness, which involves a total commitment to the practice of Dharma.

Enlightened beings, whether from long ago or in our own day can inspire admiration and then devotion. Therefore, we should take their examples sincerely to heart, and follow them by working towards Liberation for our own benefit and the benefit of all beings.

8

Mahāmudrā

The vast body of teachings we know as the Buddhadharma is traditionally said to consist of eighty-four thousand collections, and each one of these is said to contain as many texts as could be written with all the ink an elephant can carry on its back. The Buddhadharma contains an inexhaustible wealth of teachings and techniques; and every one of these has the same fundamental purpose: to benefit beings in their many conditions by helping them to understand the nature of mind.

According to the Buddhadharma, Enlightenment has three aspects (see pages 36–38). One of these is the Dharmakaya, which is often represented by the figure of Vajradhara or Dorje Chang [rdo rje 'chang]. It is from the level of awareness expressed by Dorje Chang that the teachings known as the tantras have been promulgated among human beings. In the *Secret Heart* tantra, called in Tibetan the *Sang way nying po* [gsang ba'i snying po] and in Sanskrit the *Guhyagarbha-tantra*, we find a prayer of praise to mind itself:

I pay homage to the mind
which is like a wish-fulfilling gem,
through which one can realize all one's aims.
Mind-nature is the basis for everything;
There is nothing in samsara or Nirvana that does not come from it.

The four main orders of the Buddhist tradition in Tibet—Sakyapa, Gelügpa, Kagyüpa and Nyingmapa—use many techniques of practice. Each has preliminary practices that consist initially of taking Refuge in the Three Jewels, then formalizing that commitment by acts of prostration and recitation, offering, purification, and meditations that identify us with our Lama. Each school has techniques for calming the mind and developing insight into its nature; each employs Vajrayana meditation practices that involve the stages of Development and Fulfillment. All of these many practices are geared towards deepening an authentic understanding of the nature of mind; they exist for no other purpose.

In the Kagyüpa school one of the main cycles of teaching is termed the Six Dharmas or Yogas of Naropa, six techniques through which we can begin the profound transformation of all aspects of our experience. All these techniques employ a rapid approach. They are a supremely effective path to Enlightenment, and involve Mahāmudrā meditation and the cycle of teachings concerned with the Mahāmudrā Realization.

Mahāmudrā is a Sanskrit word meaning "supreme symbol" or "supreme seal." In Tibetan it is translated as *cha ja chen po* [phyag rgya chen po]. *Cha* is an honorific word for hand, which in turn is a code word for the Emptiness of mind and all phenomena. The second syllable, *ja*, means seal, as on a document. It signifies something that gathers everything under one heading and seals it in its embrace. It refers to the all-embracing nature of Mahāmudrā Realization: no aspect of experience falls outside it, for it is the all-embracing awareness of the essential Emptiness of experience and phenomena. *Chen po* means great, and signifies that this experience is ultimate—there is nothing greater.

Mahāmudrā Realization and the teachings leading to it can be considered the quintessence of all Buddhist practice. The doctrine is profound and difficult to grasp; the experience is intangible and cannot be demonstrated to the senses. A stanza from the teaching of the Buddha praises Prajñāparamitā, the Perfection of Wisdom, who personifies this experience.

The first line says that the Perfection of Wisdom cannot be spoken about, cannot be described, cannot be conceived of. The traditional comparison is with a mute person tasting sugar: the experience cannot be communicated to anyone else. In the same way Mahāmudrā must be experienced personally to be understood: one cannot describe it clearly and effectively to another person, but one can make an attempt, and this is what the quatrain does.

The second line specifies that although realization of the nature of mind, the Perfection of Wisdom, is indescribable, we can say that it is not subject to origination or cessation. There is an eternal quality to the nature of mind, which is empty, like space.

The third line identifies the realization of mind as the province of one's own awareness; it is properly understood only in one's own awareness and experience, not in someone else's description. Primordial Awareness is the direct and authentic experience of the mind as empty, clear and unimpeded, as dynamic and intelligent. This can only be verified through personal experience and the use of one's own intelligence.

The fourth line is a personification: "I pay homage to the mother of the Buddhas of the three times." In this metaphor our realization of the nature of mind, as well as that nature itself, is described as the origin of Enlightenment, because it is through this direct Realization that we experience Buddhahood. This is how enlightened beings experienced it in the past, how they experience it now, and how they will experience it in the future. Any being that achieves, has achieved or will achieve Enlightenment, realizes the same nature of mind, personified here as the mother of the Victorious Ones, the Buddhas. As a mother gives birth to a child, so the mind, once its nature is discovered, gives birth to enlightenment. As surely as we are born from a womb, so surely can we give birth to Enlightenment by directly realizing the empty, clear and unimpeded nature of mind; other than that, there is no means. Iconographically, this supreme feminine principle is represented by such deities as Prajñāparamitā herself, Dorje Phagmo, and many others whose female forms symbolize this state of awareness, Mahāmudrā Realization.

Approaches to Mahāmudrā

In all the schools of Buddhism in Tibet, a threefold approach to the Dharma is recognized. The first stage involves intellectual study, listening to the teachings and understanding their meaning. The second stage is one of contemplating what has been learned in order to deepen one's understanding. The third stage involves meditation and direct experience of what has been understood. Given this similarity in approach, however, each school tends to develop its own style, favoring either a predominantly intellectual or academic approach, (shay pay ka bap [bshad pa'i bka' bab]), or a more intuitive, meditative one, (drup pay ka bap [sgrub pa'i bka' bab]). The Sakyapa and Gelügpa schools, in particular, are noted for their intellectual skill in the doctrine. They maintain that to attain the state of awareness, one first must understand thoroughly what has been written and taught by those who have experienced it. One therefore approaches the direct experience of mind on the basis of a very thorough and far-reaching intellectual understanding of the nature of reality, experience, mind, and so on. For such persons, the first stage of hearing involves thorough intellectual preparation.

The other, more pragmatic, meditative approach is stressed by the Kagyüpas and Nyingmapas. Although these schools do not deny the validity of an approach based on vast intellectual understanding, their view is perhaps best summed up in the words of Atiśa, who brought transmissions and teachings from India to Tibet, and from whom all lineages derive inspiration. Referring to the Indian myth of the swan that can extract pure milk from a mixture of milk and water, he said: "The field of knowledge is incredibly vast, and life is very, very short. Thus, the most important approach is to extract milk from the water, like the swan, and to practice what is most relevant to one's situation." This is the approach the Kagyüpas and Nyingmapas aspire to when they emphasize involvement in meditative development without the preliminary requirement of extensive intellectual training. There is not always enough time for that, since there is no guarantee that we shall live long enough to cover all the necessary ground. But if we can extract the essence of the teaching and apply it to our lives directly, we have a valid approach to Dharma practice.

Despite these differences in emphasis, however, all schools have the same ultimate goal, and all agree that the threefold approach of intellectual study, contemplation, and meditation is necessary for true Realization.

The intellectual approach to the three-fold process emphasizes a thorough understanding of Buddhist scriptures and commentaries on them. In the Sutra tradition, one studies the Vinaya, or rules of monastic discipline; the Sutras, or discourses; and the Abhidharma, which is sometimes termed the psychology of the Buddhist tradition. In the tantric tradition one studies the four levels of tantras, Kriya, Carya, Yoga and Anuttarayoga, the Action, Performance, Yoga, and Highest Yoga tantras. For a person taking the intuitive, meditative approach, sufficient intellectual preparation consists of first finding a qualified Lama, someone of exceptional accomplishment, to give authentic and accurate instructions in meditation technique, and, secondly, studying the technique thoroughly.

Whether we follow the scholastic or meditative approach really depends on our inclination, but regardless of how extensive or specialized our own interest may be, some intellectual basis is certainly necessary. It is said that someone who tries to meditate without a conceptual understanding of what he or she is doing is like a blind person trying to find the way in open country: such a person can only wander about, with no idea how to choose one direction over another.

On the other hand, we also have a saying that one who studies a great deal without ever applying it in meditation is like a person without hands trying to climb a rockface; one can see it, know how to get to it, know exactly what route to take, but without hands it's useless.

Although Mahāmudrā is not a vast subject, its meaning is very deep. To understand what is said about it is necessary, but not in itself sufficient. We must reflect on the teachings, and analyze them, asking, "Is this really true or not? If it is true, how and why is it true, and how do I know?" Such examination, in which the mind comes to some certainty, is the second phase of the process. Once we have recognized something in the teaching as true and valid for our situation, then we try to apply it in meditation.

The Nature of Mind

The fact that appropriate questions about the teaching arise in the mind at all indicates a considerable accumulation of merit brought about by virtuous thoughts and actions in the past. Nonetheless, we have only a vague, naive understanding of the mind. We know that we have a mind, but there is a great deal of ignorance about its nature.

What is mind, then? Mind is that which is aware, which gives rise to thoughts, emotions and feelings such as "I'm happy," or "I'm sad." Mind is what experiences all this. In Buddhism we term the nature of mind Emptiness. By this we mean that mind is devoid of, empty of, any limiting characteristics. It has no form, no color, no shape, no size, no limitation whatsoever. Analogous to this is the open space in a room. Like this space, mind is intangible and cannot be described; just as space itself is intrinsically empty — just as one never says "space is empty up to this point, while beyond it space is no longer empty" — so mind is intrinsically empty.

If we take the illumination in the room into account, we have a further analogy, because the mind has its own kind of clarity, though not in a visual sense. This illuminating capacity is mind's inherent ability to experience. No thing in and of itself, mind nevertheless experiences everything, and that ability is Clarity. We experience this when we sit quietly by ourselves and, thinking of some far away place like New York or San Francisco, find we can call it to mind immediately. In speaking of mind, then, we can refer to its Emptiness — fundamental intangibility — and to the illuminating Clarity it demonstrates. Like the space and light in the room, these are not things separate from each other, but are two aspects of a single experience.

The properties, Emptiness and Clarity, do not complete our description of mind. Mind is more than empty, illuminated space; it is also the awareness that can decide "this is form, this is sound, this is a shape." The intelligence that allows us to make judgments and recognize particular details is a manifestation of mind's Unimpededness.

Although the mind's Emptiness, Clarity and Unimpededness are inseparable, we can examine it from different perspectives, and speak of them separately or in combination. The mind's essential Emptiness and its clear nature taken together are what we call its Unimpededness, its power to experience. The fundamental threefold nature of mind — empty, clear and unimpeded — is Tathāgatagarbha, the Seed of Enlightenment, possessed by every living being, human or otherwise. Tathāgatagarbha is the fundamental purity of the mind's intrinsic nature. In the words of the Buddha Shakyamuni: "This Tathāgatagarbha, this Seed for Enlightenment, pervades all forms of life. There is not a single being that does not have it." A tantric text states that all beings are innately enlightened but that adventitious obscurations block the experience of Enlightenment. If through practice we begin to recognize the inherent nature of mind we can become completely enlightened.

The Nature of Experience

Although the concept that mind is empty of any limiting characteristic may be at least superficially understandable, many people find great difficulty in the idea that what we experience is likewise empty. What does it mean to say that the phenomenal world — this animate and inanimate universe we perceive — is empty? How is that true for this world full of rocks and trees and houses, earth, water and all the elements, living creatures moving about living their lives?

There is actually no contradiction in saying that something that appears to be so real is essentially empty. We can illustrate this by an example, the dream state.

When we go to sleep at night we dream. The mind is active in the dream, there is perception of form that is seen, sound that is heard, odors that are smelled, tastes that are tasted, textures that are felt, thoughts that arise. All these happen in the dream state, but when we wake it is obvious that nothing real was experienced. What occurred had a conventional reality during the dream, but no one will maintain that what took place in the dream happened in the same way things happen in our waking state. The dream was a series of mental projections: it had a conventional, temporary reality, but not an ultimate one. Because the dream lacks an enduring self-nature, we can say that it is empty.

We can think of our perception of the waking world in just such a way. All sorts of ideas, emotions, concepts and reactions arise in us. Things we experience can make us happy, sad, or angry, can increase our attachment or aversion. But even though all these thoughts and responses arise, none has any nature of its own: we should not take them to be real—they are simply ongoing mental projections produced by particular circumstances. For this reason we can again say that our experience is empty, because it lacks any ultimate self-nature. We can say that no aspect of our experience, of the outer phenomenal world or the inner mental world, has one atom of reality. Nothing we experience is anything more than the mind's perception of its own projections, the reality of which is only conventional.

By understanding this and coming to experience it, teachers such as Milarepa can demonstrate miracles and make things happen contrary to the normal laws that govern the universe. If the universe were something ultimately real in its own right, its laws would be inviolable, and miraculous events impossible. In fact, the laws governing conventional reality are flexible, and once we realize this we have at least some limited power to manipulate the phenomenal world.

If it is the case that all experience is only the projection of mind, what determines the way in which our perceptions take place? The force that influences the way in which mind experiences the world is karma, actions and their results.

On the basis of fundamental ignorance about the real nature of mind, karmic tendencies and other obscurations develop. The fundamental state of unawareness is like the earth, in which seeds can be planted. The seeds represent karmic predispositions, which are reinforced by physical, mental and verbal actions. Once a seed is planted, it needs support from the earth, and nourishment, water, light, heat: without these, it remains inert. When all the requisite circumstances are present, the seed germinates, grows, flowers and multiplies. In the same way, the tendency established and reinforced by an action is stored in the fundamental state of confusion and remains latent until circumstances in the environment or in the mind itself provide a channel by which the tendency emerges and comes to fruition as an active part of our experience.

As human beings we exist in a relatively superior state. This is a result of positive karmic tendencies reinforced by virtuous ac-tions — mental, verbal and physical — in countless previous lifetimes. All human karma is similar enough for all of us to experience more or less the same world: we have engaged in actions that result in similar, if not identical, impressions of what the world is like.

In addition to this general karma, there is also individual kar-ma, which accounts for the particular variations in the experience of each and every being. To be greedy or to steal establishes a tendency which, if reinforced, results in experiences of poverty and want, often in a future lifetime. On the other hand, to be generous, materially or otherwise, establishes conditions which, if reinforced, result in prosperity. Deliberate acts of killing establish a tendency which, if reinforced, results in a great deal of sickness and shortness of life, whereas to protect and respect life is conducive to good health and longevity. In short, while human beings share general qualities that are common to the human condition, some are richer or poorer than others, happier or unhappier, healthier or unhealthier, longer or shorter lived.

So, karma has both general and specific aspects, which together account for our group and individual experience. To understand the nature of that experience, however, and how the karmic process of cause and effect works, we have to understand the nature of mind. To understand the nature of mind, and to attain direct experience of it — Mahāmudrā Realization — we have to meditate.

In Mahāmudrā practice there is an advanced level of realiza-tion called *ro chik* [ro gcig] in Tibetan, meaning "one taste." At this point the sameness of subject and object becomes apparent, and causality becomes empirically obvious. We can *see* a given cause leading to a given effect.

How is it that we do not have this experience already? What prevents us from directly apprehending the nature of mind right now? There are four basic reasons, the Four Faults.

The first reason is that for us the mind is *too close* (nye drak [nye drags]) to be recognized. Since the moment we were born and began using our eyes, we have never seen our own faces directly. In our present situation mind can experience anything but cannot see its own nature.

The second reason is that the experience is *too profound* (sap drak [zab drags]) for us to fathom. We are like people looking at the surface of the ocean: we guess it to be deep, but we have no idea how deep it actually is. If we could fathom Mahāmudrā, we would be enlightened, because to fathom it would be to realize it and to realize it means to be a Buddha.

The third reason is that Mahāmudrā is *too easy* (la drak [sla drags]) for us to believe. For someone who has really understood and experienced it, Mahāmudrā is the easiest thing in the world. There is nothing to do: we don't have to cross oceans to get to it, there are no mountains to climb. The only thing necessary is bare awareness of the ultimate nature of mind, which is always there. Beyond that, there is nothing to do—but we really can't believe Mahāmudrā can be so easy to do, or rather not do. It requires only that we rest in the nature of mind.

The fourth reason is that enlightenment is *too excellent* (zang drak [bzang drags]) for us to accommodate. Buddhahood is the complete unfolding of the mind's infinite potential, which can take an infinite number of different forms and has qualities we never find in an ordinary person. The immense potential of Buddhahood doesn't fit into our narrow way of thinking, and we really cannot accommodate the notion that such a state is the real nature of our mind.

Given these difficulties, what must we do to experience the nature of mind directly? There are two fundamental elements in this transformation: (1) our own efforts to purify evil actions and obscurations, and to develop merit and awareness; and (2) devotion to our Lama, who plays an indispensable part in bringing about our transformation. These two elements together bring about Mahāmudrā Realization.

The pure, fundamental nature of mind, without confusion or obscuration, is known as Co-emergent Primordial Awareness (len che ye she [lhen skyes ye shes]). Primordial Awareness, inherently the nature of mind, and free of obscuring factors, is co-emergent with consciousness (nam she [rnam shes]). One text tells us that the only means of realizing Co-emergent Primordial Awareness are our own efforts in purifying faults and developing merit and awareness and our devoion to and reliance on a qualified Lama. Any other approach is a waste of time. These two elements, of effort and devotion, must go together, and that is why they are combined in physical practices like prostration, verbal practices like prayer and mantra, and mental practices like visualization and meditation. To use these faculties is to eliminate the fourth karmic level of obscuration; we counterbalance negative tendencies, and eventually remove them as sources of confusion. Specifically, through *shi nay* meditation we develop stability or calmness of mind; that means that our mind can rest in a given state without distraction or confusion. At that point we begin to eliminate the third level of obscuration, emotional afflictions.

The next phase of meditation is insight into the nature of mind using the techniques of *lha tong*. This is often called the experience of selflessness which has two aspects: the absence of a personal self, and the non-existence of all phenomena as independent entities. We begin to realize that the self and the objects we perceive as external lack any ultimate reality. With experience of this insight, the second obscuration is eliminated, that of the habitual tendencies to dualistic clinging.

Now through the practices of Mahāmudrā meditation we move from a state of ignorance to a state of direct perception and experience of the fundamental nature of mind. When ignorance has been transformed into Primordial Awareness the first, most subtle level of obscuration, the obscuration of the fundamental ignorance, is removed. This is complete Enlightenment.

These terms and practices seem formidable, but this is not to say that it necessarily requires a great deal of work to attain enlightenment and realize Mahāmudrā. It depends on circumstances. If a person has matured through lifetimes of purification and development, with a great accumulation of Merit and Awareness, then an instantaneous transformation can take place when a skillful, enlightened teacher is met.

Devotion to the Lama

An important stage in the practice of Mahāmudrā is meditation upon the Lama, who is conceived of as the union of all blessing
and inspiration. The teacher is visualized either in the sky in front of
us or on the crown of the head. We pray one-pointedly for the
Lama's blessing, and afterwards meditate that the form of the guru
dissolves into us. Thereafter, we simply let the mind rest in its
natural state. By that point we actually are in Mahāmudrā meditation.

The importance of the Lama is characteristic of the Vajrayana,
and is not found in the Hinayana or Mahayana. It is true that pray-
ing to the Buddhas and Bodhisattvas and taking Refuge in them is
an effective way to attain Enlightenment, but it is more gradual
than the Vajrayana way of establishing a working relationship with a
Lama. The Vajrayana contains teachings that can take one to the
experience of complete Enlightenment in this lifetime. The Lama is
the one who bestows those teachings. That is why the Lama is so
crucial in tantric practice, and why Mahāmudrā teachings, which
are part of tantric practice, place such emphasis on the student's
relationship with the Lama.

Someone of the highest abiltities, engaged in Mahāmudrā
practice, has intense faith in his or her Lama, and intense compassion for all other beings. He or she understands that while every sentient being has the potential to become enlightened, all the confusion and obscurations preventing the direct experience of mind
create endless suffering and frustration. That understanding is the
source of compassion. In all practice of Dharma, whatever technique or meditation is employed, taking Refuge with great faith
should be followed by the development of Bodhicitta.

Every Buddha who has achieved Enlightenment in the past has
done so through first giving rise to Bodhicitta, the deep wish that
our practice be not only for our own benefit, but for the benefit and
eventual Enlightenment of every sentient being. In fact, it is because
we are so concerned with our own interests, and so little with others'
welfare, that we continue to wander in confusion, reinforcing our
involvement with samsara. That is why concern for the happiness
and Liberation of others is crucial to Dharma practice.

Finally, this best type of person has intense dedication and diligence in practice, so that any task required is carried through with ardor. If all these qualities come together in the practitioner, a very rare transformation can take place. Most people, however, are not of such superior capabilities. How does someone, matured through previous lifetimes, but still at a lower level of preparation, go about attaining ultimate awareness? Just as clouds keep us from seeing the sun, thick levels of obscuration in our mind keep us unaware of the nature of mind. The function of our practice is to dispel those obscurations until direct experience of the mind can take place.

You need not give up in despair, thinking, "It's hopeless. I have so many obscurations it will take me lifetimes to get rid of them." We are not meant to feel like that. Rapid transformation is the purpose of the wonderfully effective teachings of the Buddha. If you practice regularly, even for a few hours, even a few minutes, you can eliminate the confusions and obscurations that took aeons to accumulate. That is the special blessing and efficacy of the Dharma.

Practice

For Mahāmudrā meditation to develop properly, our physical posture should be as straight as possible — not tense or rigid but erect and relaxed. In fact, relaxation of body, speech and mind is very important in meditation. With reference to speech, the jaws should not be clenched, nor should any of the associated muscles be tight. The lips should not be moving. The mind should not be tense or forced in any particular direction.

Once we have assumed a properly relaxed posture, we can try the following technique, searching for the "Origin, Location, and Direction" of mind, (jung nay dro sum ['byung gnas 'gro gsum]). In this context mind means that which experiences everything we perceive, think, and feel. Being aware of this mind, we inquire: Where does it come from? Can we find any origin for it? And where is mind located? Is it anywhere inside or outside the body? Is it located in any physical organ, any particular part of the body? Or is it in the external world? When the mind moves, does it actually go anywhere?

Does mind move in any particular direction? If so, how does it move? As long as the mind is at rest, simply dwelling in a state of clear, transparent awareness without any thought, what rests and what experiences that rest is nothing other than mind itself. When a thought arises, the mind adopts some form of expression, takes some direction. How does that come about? In this technique, we try to maintain awareness of the process by which thought arises and takes form; we try to understand the nature of the actual experience of thought arising in the mind. The point is not whether the thought is a good or bad one. We are not concerned with the content of the thought, but the nature of it. How does a thought arise in the mind? Having arisen, where is it? How and where does it stay? When it disappears, what direction does it go in? North, south, east, west, up, down? Where does it disappear to? What is the cessation of a thought?

When there is no thought in the mind, but the mind is resting in a state of clear undistracted awareness, where exactly is it? Can we locate the mind anywhere? How does the mind dwell when it dwells in this state? When we examine the mind at rest, does it have any size of shape or limiting characteristic that we can discern and define?

In this approach, then, we seek to understand the mind in terms of its origin, location and direction. In its arising, staying, and passing away, is there anything we can describe other than empty, clear and unimpeded mind? Exactly how would we describe it?

If we use this technique again and again until there is some certainty about what constitutes mind and how it works, it is entirely possible that we will come to some degree of authentic realization. On the other hand, there is also the danger of fooling ourselves, of getting lost in our own confusion and coming to what we think is a definite understanding when in fact we really have not understood anything. This is precisely where a relationship with a qualified meditation teacher is important. We need someone who can explain the process, evaluate our experiences, and give advice. If we refine our meditative technique in this way, by our own efforts and with the help of a skillful teacher's advice, our experience will become stable and authentic.

It is traditionally said that when mind is not contrived it is spontaneously blissful, just as water, when not agitated, is by nature transparent and clear. This is a most accurate description. In Mahāmudrā meditation we should maintain a bare awareness of the nature of mind as it is, without any effort to force some particular state of consciousness, to contrive a particular experience. In that sense, the goal is to be totally relaxed in a state of naked awareness, without distraction or dullness, alert to the nature of mind.

When the mind is resting in such a state and a thought arises, has the mind which was at rest become the mind in action? Or has something else been added to the mind that was at rest, something separate from mind? Are mind and thought the same? These are questions we need to be aware of while meditating.

When the mind is resting in this clear state of undistracted awareness, without any actual thoughts arising, the capacity that is aware of that state of being (and which is aware of mind in motion when mind is active and thoughts arise) is the mind's own Awareness. Are the mind at rest, the mind in motion, and the mind's Awareness different or identical?

These questions belong to another approach recognized in the Mahāmudrā tradition known as "The States of Rest, Movement, and Awareness," (nay ju rik sum [gnas 'gyu rig gsum]). If you work with this approach and come to what you feel is a significant experience, you can then consult the Lama whose judgment will help you determine whether it is authentic or not, and whether or not you are working in the right direction. As in the previous approach, a certain "pointing out" (ngo trö [ngo sprod]) of your experience by a skillful Lama will be very beneficial.

Mistakes and Misunderstandings

If you understand the nature of these teachings and practice them well, there is perhaps no single more effective approach to the attainment of complete Enlightenment. But without understanding and effective practice, you are open to all sorts of errors. Without thorough understanding you may overemphasize one aspect or another of the teaching and thus distort it. For example, you might isolate the statement that phenomena, mind and experience are all empty, and develop a nihilistic view, thinking that nothing matters because everything is empty; that karma, virtuous and non-virtuous action, Enlightenment, and non-enlightenment do not exist. This is perhaps the single most harmful wrong view you could possibly develop.

It is true, of course, that the teachings say that mind and all experience are empty. But the proper approach is to understand first the subjective nature of experience — that everything we perceive of the outer world, the physical body and the inner workings of our mind, is a projection and expression of mind. Having understood that, we return to the mind to determine that it is indeed essentially empty of limiting characteristics. But simply to understand this is not enough. You have to experience it through meditation. Only then, when you have directly realized the emptiness of mind and all experience, might you perhaps say: "Now I am not subject to the karmic process, the causal relationship between action and experience." Until you have had the direct realization of Emptiness that cuts the karmic process, karma is still unfailing and inescapable. Positive deeds will continue to give rise to positive results, and negative deeds give rise to negative ones. This is not something you can change in any way. It is simply the way the karmic process unfolds as long as you have not had the Realization of the Emptiness of mind and all experience.

In following the Mahāmudrā path of meditation, there are many other possibilities for error. For example, if the mind lacks alertness, the result is not pure meditation at all, but stupidity. To reinforce this situation by taking it as the basis of meditative experience leads to rebirth in the desire realm as an animal, especially one given to lethargy, like a crocodile, or creature that hibernates for months on end.

Even positive signs in the development of our meditation can become obstacles. In Mahāmudrā practice we can distinguish three basic forms of positive experience: states of bliss (de wa [bde ba]), states of clarity (sal wa [gsal ba]), and states of non-conceptual awareness (mi tok pa [mi rtog pa]).

If, for example, an experience of bliss arises and we cling to it or reinforce it, we fall into an error of limitation. Such practice will definitely contribute to a higher rebirth, among the gods of the Desire Realm, for example. But the meditation is unstable, and its results subject to exhaustion; it will not take us to a pure state of Realization beyond the cycle of rebirth.

If experiences of clarity arise, clinging to them leads to rebirth in one or another of the seventeen levels of gods in the Form Realm, still in the cycle of samsara. Should the experience of non-conceptual awareness arise in meditation, and Emptiness itself become an object of clinging, this kind of meditation, if reinforced, will still lead to rebirth in one or another of the four levels of the Formless Realm of samsara, and we will remain in the cycle of conditioned existence.

Such errors are possible until we actually attain Liberation from samsara. It is, therefore, important not to abandon the practice of purifying ourselves by eliminating negative tendencies and developing positive ones such as compassion, wholesome aspiration, and so on. All these are very important.

Perhaps the best way to conclude this brief introduction to Mahāmudrā is with the words of Tilopa when his student, the great pandit Naropa, had his first experience of Mahāmudrā Realization under Tilopa's guidance:

"Naropa, my son, never be separate from practices which develop your Merit and deepen your Awareness. Merit and Awareness are like the two wheels on the chariot that is taking you to Enlightenment."

Questions and Answers

QUESTION: If mind is intrinsically pure, where do obscurations come from?

ANSWER: In Buddhism, we do not try to ascribe an origin to ignorance. We do not say that at some point the mind became unable to see itself and lost the direct experience of its own pure nature. Rather, we speak of the beginningless cycle of existence, and accept that as long as there was mind, there was ignorance, co-emergent (len chik che wa [lhan gcig skyes ba]) with mind itself. As mind arises, so does ignorance, and in our present state we cannot speak of mind separate from ignorance. Further distortion takes place; the essential Emptiness of mind is distorted into a subjective leaning toward something that appears existent in itself. Rather than experiencing directly the essential Emptiness of mind, we experience a self.

Buddhist texts do not exaggerate when they say that our greatest enemy is clinging to a self. Why? We are caught in a situation where mind is incapable of directly experiencing its own essential emptiness, and instead posits a self that must be sustained. We thus develop all the needs and wants that must be gratified in order to maintain such a self. Suffering comes from the endless search to satisfy that which cannot be satisfied. "I" leads to "I am" which leads to "I want" and so on.

The fundamental level of ignorance, the first level of obscuration in the mind, is the mind's inability to recognize its own nature. Moreover, mind is not simply empty. It has another aspect, its Clarity, which is its ability to experience all sensory impressions, thoughts, emotions and ideas. Because of fundamental ignorance, this aspect of the mind is also taken to be something different: the objects we perceive are seen not as expressions of the mind's Clarity, but as existent in and of themselves, separate from the mind. A dualistic split has occurred between the self which is posited, and an object understood to be separate from it. This duality and the clinging to it is the obscuration of habitual tendencies, the second level of mental obscuration.

Thus in our present situation, we already have a degree of ignorance which causes us to experience a self as something ultimately real. Further, the Clarity of mind has been distorted into something objective, seen as completely separate from the mind and ultimately real.

This condition will continue forever if we do not attain Enlightenment. We cannot expect it simply to fade away. On the contrary, if we do not transcend the obscurations which led to this distortion, the state is permanent. It will continue to reinforce itself as long as we do not attain Enlightenment.

Even when we go to sleep, this dualism carries over from the waking state. In an entirely different realm, where the projections of the mind arise in dreams, there is still the perception of "I" and "other," the self and something outside it. This division permits all the other more complex aspects of the dream state, such as pleasure, happiness, pain and so on.

In the future, when each of us comes to die, and our physical bodies are gone, even in that totally disembodied state, where there can be no physical basis for consciousness, there is a continued impression of embodiment, and the dualistic habit of mind continues: experiences arising in the mind are projected into an environment, and experienced as something other than mind itself.

The third aspect of mind is its Unimpededness. In a pure state this is simply the mind's spontaneous cognitive activity, but when we are caught in the split between subject and object, the thought arises, "That object is good, I want it," and so attraction and attachment form. Or we think, "That threatens me, that's bad," and repulsion and aversion develop. There is also another possibility — that of simple stupidity, of not understanding the situation at all, but being caught up in the whole illusion. The three fundamental poisons or patterns of emotional reaction — attachment, aversion and stupidity — enter here, and from them develops an abundance of emotions, which we traditionally call the eighty-four thousand emotions that afflict the mind. The distortion of the Unimpededness of mind forms the third level of obscuration, the obscuration of emotional afflictions.

When we speak about the three realms of the universe — the Desire, Form and Formless Realms — we are talking about the distorted side of the pure nature of mind, which itself is essentially empty, clear in nature and unobstructed in manifestation.

What pertains on the general level to the universe also applies to the individual unenlightened being: the experience of a self is a distorted perception of the direct experience of the essential emptiness of mind; the experience of speech is the distorted perception of the clear nature of mind; and the experience of the physical body is the distorted perception of the unimpeded manifestation of mind. With this threefold distortion we produce not only samsaric existence in general, but also the body, speech, and mind of an individual being.

Because of these distortions, we behave in various ways. Physically, verbally and mentally, we react through emotional affliction, which through repetition becomes habitual. Once habits are established, they lead to yet further actions which, like all actions, lead to specific results later on. Causality connects our experiences with our actions. This is karmic obscuration. In this way, our basic confusion, our ignorance of the fundamental nature of mind is harmful to ourselves and others.

We can think of these four levels of confusion (fundamental ignorance, duality, emotional afflictions, unskillful action) as dependent upon one another. Basic ignorance is the mind's failure to experience the Primordial Awareness which is its own nature. From this fundamental ignorance develops the dualistic clinging to self and others as separate, independent entities. This is the second level of obscuration. The third level of obscuration, the mental afflictions, emerge from dualistic clinging. Finally, based upon emotional afflictions, the fourth level, karmic obscuration, develops, wherein all these unskillful, negative tendencies are reinforced through physical, verbal and mental actions.

In our present condition as unenlightened beings, we experience all four levels at the same time. The inherent purity of mind has not been lost, but it is so veiled that we experience a great mass of obscuration. Confusion covers the pure nature of the mind as clouds cover the sun. The single element binding all this confusion together is the clinging to the reality of a self.

Until all these levels of confusion and obscuration are eliminated, Enlightenment cannot arise. We must recover the original purity and transparency of water now polluted by sediment; we must disperse the clouds veiling the sun, so we can see clearly and receive its warmth directly. Once we understand through meditation the Emptiness of mind, its Clarity and Unimpededness, the intense constriction produced by clinging to self and phenomena begins to diminish.

QUESTION: My emotions seem as real as my body and the world around me. They interfere with my practice. What can I do about it?

ANSWER: At present, we are instinctively sure that we exist and have a mind. We are intensely aware of the physical body. We think, *my body*, and tend to regard the two, body and mind, as one. So we tend to experience emotions on the physical and mental levels simultaneously, as if they were somehow inherent in both. In fact, the origin of all emotion is mental. Ultimately speaking, the way these emotions arise in the mind has nothing to do with the body. We have simply conditioned the mind to experience them as if there were some physical origin for any emotion. In fact, the mind is like a stern king, and the body like a humble servant. It is the body's function to follow the orders of the mind, which it does without any identity of its own. If there were no desire in the mind, there would be none in the body. Likewise, if the mind is without anger, so is the body.

Our problem now is that we experience mind and body as a unity, so whatever comes up in the mind we wish to translate immediately into physical action. When desire or anger arise in the mind, we hurry to express it on a physical level. Our sole mode of experience seems to be that emotions arise in mind and body simultaneously. Yet this is not the case. If it were, then when the mind and body are separated at death, the corpse would continue to feel desire and anger, and act accordingly.

What is necessary is to understand how emotions arise in the mind, and how the physical body is based upon the projection of mind. We must understand more about the nature of mind itself, and see the intangibility of thoughts and emotions that arise from an essentially empty state of mind.

Since thoughts and emotions — attachment, aversion, envy, pride, and so on — are insubstantial and intangible, then we need not go to all the trouble of expressing them physically or verbally. Even if we do not have direct meditative experience, a great deal of difficulty can be eliminated simply by intellectually understanding that mental projections are as intangible and empty as mind itself. Nagarjuna, the great Indian siddha and scholar, said:

All things are realized when Emptiness is realized.
Nothing is realized when Emptiness is not realized.

If one has this basic understanding of the Emptiness of mind and its projections, then any method of meditation will be effective. Without it, no technique will work.

QUESTION: Doesn't the desire for Enlightenment contradict the teachings that say desire is a bad thing?

ANSWER: We have to want Enlightenment, because we must start from where we are right now — afflicted with a great deal of dualistic attachment. Since our experiences are governed by a sense of "I" and that "I" therefore wants "things," let us at least make what we want something worthy — Enlightenment. As we actually get closer to that Enlightenment, the need to want it becomes less powerful. As we progress through the first, second and third Bodhisattva levels, we experience an increasing awareness of the Emptiness of the self, and of the true nature of mind. This brings a gradual lessening of our desire for Enlightenment.

We can illustrate this rather simply. When you started this morning from wherever you were in New York to come here, you first had the strong thought in your mind, "I'm going to the teaching." The closer you got, the less you needed to worry about it, because you were getting closer. When you finally arrived here, there was no point in thinking, "I've got to get to the teaching," because you had already arrived. Dualistic desire for Enlightenment is gradually dispelled and need not be considered an obstacle; in a certain way, it is essential.

QUESTION: How can one practice Mahāmudrā if one does not have regular contact with one's Lama?

ANSWER: If we are not able to be in close proximity to our Lama, it does not mean that we cannot receive blessing and inspiration and guidance from that teacher. If we really have faith in our teacher, it does not matter how far away we are or how seldom we see our Lama. It is our own faith, devotion and prayers which bring about the benefits. If such faith is lacking, we could sleep at the Lama's feet and derive no benefit.

QUESTION: When I try to meditate, my mind keeps wandering. What should I do?

ANSWER: In order to meditate properly, it is necessary to have practiced *shi nay*, tranquility meditation. This will pacify all disturbing emotions and allow your mind to remain in one-pointedness.

When you first start tranquility meditation, the experience is like water rushing from a mountain top: the mind just keeps running, full of many thoughts. Later, at the second stage, the mind is like the same river when it reaches the plains, running slowly and steadily. Later still, in the last stage, the water in the river reaches the sea and dissolves into it.

Diligence and devotion will help you calm the mind in this way, and then you will be able to meditate properly.

QUESTION: I'm not very strong physically, and it's difficult or impossible for me to sit cross-legged, let alone do prostrations and so on. Does that mean I can't learn to meditate?
ANSWER: For people who are young and healthy, it's important to keep strict meditation posture; the physical discipline will help strengthen both the body and the meditation. But older people, or those in poor health, or with some infirmity, can do their meditation in many different postures, even lying down. The meditator is mind, not body. So if you can properly meditate with the mind, your meditation will be fine.

QUESTION: I have so many responsibilities in my life that I don't have much time for practice. What should I do?
ANSWER: There is a story in Tibet about two young men. One was quite intelligent and had thought a lot about samsara, and about the enlightened state, and what these two conditions meant. The other had a basic understanding that the world was not such a good place, that Dharma practice was very good; beyond that, he did not have a clear understanding of the situation at all. Once the intelligent fellow and he were talking and he said, "Dharma practice really seems difficult, it's something you've got to put your mind to. It takes too much effort. It really is hard and bothersome to commit yourself to it." His friend answered, "It's not so difficult. You accumulate virtue and evil all the time, in everything you do; just as you walk along, what you say or what you do with your hands can be acts of virtue. Simply walking can take the life of some creature, if you step on an insect and kill it. We're always involved with virtue and non-virtue. Virtue doesn't have to be a huge project — you can simply be aware of what you're doing at each and every moment."

As you walk along, if you come to a garden which is particularly beautiful, your experience of its beauty can be an offering to the Three Jewels or to your Lama. It can be offered with the sincere intention that thereby all beings may develop merit, deepen

Awareness, and progress on the Path. In this way an ordinary aesthetic experience can be transformed into an offering which your motivation can make very great, very powerful. If you meet an animal, you can do something very simple, like saying OM MANI PADME HUNG so it hears the sound; some seed has been planted. That takes no effort beyond repeating those six syllables, yet it is beneficial.

QUESTION: What are indications that higher levels of Realization are being reached? What happens?
ANSWER: Through Realization, freedom of mind increases. That's really all that takes place, but this freedom expresses itself in a variety of ways.

Imagine a hundred different images of the Buddha, each showing a multiplicity of colors, postures and so on, in a hundred different places around the world—India, China, America, Canada, France and so on. Imagine trying to meditate on all these varied images of the Buddha simultaneously. We would be doing well to visualize even one clearly. This is because our present mind is so limited. At the first of the ten Bodhisattva levels, mind can encompass all those one hundred objects of meditation in a single instant without confusion, with no detail missing. This is freedom of mind.

As this freedom of mind begins to express itself, it retains certain limitations, but its capacity is far greater than what we experience now. A story may illustrate this. A Mahasiddha named Jalandhara held a particular lineage of the *Hevajra Tantra.* He gave a disciple the empowerment and meditation instruction for visualizing the form of the Yidam Hevajra. Then Jalandhara sent him into retreat.

Now Hevajra has sixteen arms and is quite a complex figure. The disciple meditated on this form and identified himself with it in meditation. He attained success in his practice to the extent that he felt he was the Yidam and could in actuality manifest those sixteen arms. At that point Jalandhara came to see how his student was doing. When he got there he said, "You should wash my feet." India is often very hot and dusty, so that when someone comes to visit after a long journey, it is a mark of respect and courtesy to wash the visitor's feet in cool water. Indeed the Lama did seem hot, tired and dusty from the trip. The student brought the water in a basin to wash his Lama's feet. The Lama said, "Wash my feet; use one hand for each foot." So with his left hand the disciple began to wash Jalandhara's right foot and with his right hand the Lama's left foot. All of a sudden he looked down and the guru had four feet. That posed no problem. He simply emanated two more hands and washed the four feet. Then there were eight feet. Again no problem; he emanated eight hands. Then there were sixteen feet, so he emanated sixteen hands. All at once, though, he found himself looking down at thirty-two feet, and then he was stuck: he had treated his meditation on sixteen hands as so real, so substantial, that he couldn't get beyond that number.

QUESTION: Is the discussion of Emptiness unique to the Mahāmudrā teachings?
ANSWER: The doctrine of Emptiness is fundamental to Buddhist teachings. In the Prajñāparamitā, the literature dealing with the Perfection of Wisdom, we find detailed analyses of Emptiness from different viewpoints. Eighteen aspects of Emptiness are enumerated to facilitate an understanding of the Emptiness of phenomena and of mind.

In both Japanese and Tibetan traditions, we find great emphasis on the principle of Emptiness, and on experiencing it in meditation. In both traditions the *Heart Sutra* is chanted. The languages differ, but the essential concepts remain:

> There is no eye, there is no ear, there is no nose, there is
> no tongue, there is no body, there is no mind.

Here is a denial of the ultimate reality of all aspects of our experience. At face value, it seems absurd. Here is a monk solemnly reciting that he has no eyes, no tongue, no ears — and he patently has them. What is he talking about?

Think of a dream. In dreams we hear, see, taste, smell, touch, and think, yet no sense organs are being used. The mind relays the impression of sensory experience, but there are no sense organs involved. One wakes up and the scene disappears. Later, we treat the memory as something the mind invented. If we extend that analysis to the waking state, we will understand that all phenomena and experiences are essentially like those in dreams in that they partake of the same illusory nature. When we meditate, we will run into difficulties if we lack a basic understanding of Emptiness and the intangibility of ideas and emotions. That is why the Perfection of Wisdom teachings were given by the Buddha, and why the Wisdom sutra is still recited.

Consider someone working with a meditation practice such as that of Chenrezi. Meditating on the form of Chenrezi, we visualize ourselves in that form. When we lie down to go to sleep, does the Bodhisattva also lie down and go to sleep? Meditators can make problems like this for themselves if they treat appearances as substantial or self-existent. Once they have apprehended the Emptiness of mind, however, no such confusions occur. Emptiness does not get up or lie down. It is not subject to limitations. There is an immense freedom in the way one can use the mind through the understanding that it is essentially empty.

The *Heart Sutra* concludes wiah a mantra, TAYATA OM GATE GATE PARAGATE PARASAMGATE BODHI SOHA, which is the mantra of the Perfection of Wisdom, a mantra which pacifies all suffering. It condenses the experience of Emptiness into a verbal formula. The mantra signifies the experience of Emptiness: there is no basis from which suffering can arise, because one has seen the essential Emptiness of mind and all its experiences.

QUESTION: Rinpoche has spoken about conventional and ultimate reality. Doesn't such designation just reinforce dualistic thinking?
ANSWER: Until we have directly experienced the ultimate non-reality of self, of mind, and of causality, it is very important to accept both reality and non-reality. That is, until we are enlightened, we have to adopt two stances. We can take the position that all phenomena are ultimately unreal, even now. Since they are ultimately unreal and essentially empty, all phenomena are only conventionally real; they are not ultimate but deeply and mutually interrelated. This is the Dependent Origination of all things. On the other hand, it is essential to respect the way things work on the conventional level, because we are still bound to it. Once we achieve the

ultimate level, it will be pointless to talk about conventional or ultimate — we will be beyond both terms, beyond any dualistic mode of thought. Until we get to that stage, however, it is beneficial to accept the ultimate non-reality of phenomena, and also to acknowledge the unfailing conventional reality of things.

QUESTION: Does the intelligence of mind *produce* the thoughts of which it becomes aware?
ANSWER: If we posit a watcher, such as intelligence watching the thoughts it creates, we split the mind from what it produces; and if we posit such an initial dualism, we can compound it into an infinite series of watchers watching watchers. The mind isn't like that.

In the same way that this light source, this lamp beside me, is spontaneously expressed by the light it radiates, so the mind, which is essentially empty and clear by nature immediately and spontaneously comes to expression as mental activity. Intelligence is simply that aspect of mind which is simultaneous with mental activity, and aware of it: what arises in the mind *is* the awareness, mind radiating its spontaneous activity.

QUESTION: What connection is there between Mahāmudrā Realization and compassion?
ANSWER: Through understanding the nature of your own mind, you begin to understand more about the situation of every being in samsara. This kind of understanding, automatically and without any effort at all, gives rise to compassion for every other living being. Appreciating the nature of mind in general, you also come to understand in particular the way mind operates on the impure and the pure levels. Through understanding the impure and the pure as two aspects of the same mind, you give rise to compassion for beings trapped in the impure state of experience, and to faith in beings who have realized pure states of Awareness. There is an automatic development of faith and conviction in the Buddhas and Bodhisattva, and in the goal of Enlightenment for the sake of all beings.

Moreover, by understanding the nature of mind, you will be better able to deal with the sufferings, fears and frustrations you encounter. Once you have this basic understanding, you can deal with everything more effectively. For example, suppose you had a large, painful boil on the back of your hand. You could try various remedies: massaging it, or gently rubbing cream into it, and over a period of time you might cure it. Or, you could take a needle, lance the boil and remove the pus immediately. Whereas other kinds of practice are like a gentle, slow, and gradual approach, understanding the nature of mind cuts directly to the core of the problem. Why? Because you come to understand that all thoughts and emotions, all fears and mental turmoil are nothing but a projection of the mind.

Epilogue:

The Eight Thoughts

Through the power of the compassionate Truth of the Supreme Refuges, and through the root of virtuous action, and through pure noble motivation, may I alone, by my own efforts, dispel the sufferings, whatever they may be, of all beings, who pervade space.

Through the excellence of virtuous activity in this world and beyond it, may I fulfill the hopes and desires of beings just as they conceive them.

May my body, flesh, blood, skin, and all the rest of me benefit all sentient beings in appropriate ways.

May the sufferings of beings, who all have been my mothers, dissolve into me; may my happiness and virtue be obtained by them.

As long as the world remains, may there not arise in my mind, even for an instant, the thought of harming others.

May I exert myself diligently in benefitting beings, not letting up for even a moment because of sadness or fatigue or anything similar.

May I be able to give effortlessly whatever enjoyment is desired to all beings who are thirsty and hungry and needy and poor.

May I take upon myself the great burdens, the difficult-to-bear sufferings of beings in hell and others, and may they be liberated.

This aspiration prayer, *The Eight Thoughts of a Great Person,* was made by Karma Rangjung Kunchab [Kalu Rinpoche].

Kalu Rinpoche and Lama Norlha

Appendix 1

The Five Skandhas

by Lama Norlha

Because of the practical importance of understanding the five *skandhas*—the constituents of our experience—the editors asked Lama Norlha, the director of Kalu Rinpoche's New York retreat center, to give a teaching on them. Here Lama Norlha gives a concise account of the *skandhas*, and integrates with it teachings that suggest how the information may be used in meditation.

At the end of the article is a tabular outline of the *skandhas*, with the Tibetan terminology.

All the teachings presented by the Buddha in the sutras, whether they deal with the Basis for the Path, the Path itself, or the Fruit of the Path, can be subsumed under the topic of the five *skandhas* (pung bo nga [phung po lnga]). The study of the five skandhas is important because it directly relates to our habitual tendency to cling to a self.

Skandha, a Sanskrit word, means 'heap' or aggregate, and refers to the objects and mental states of which our experience is composed. There are five: Form, Sensation, Recognition, Formation, and Consciousness.

Form (zuk [gzugs])

The first, form, is a very general term referring to all the many things perceivable by the eye and other sense organs, whether they be near or far, clear or indistinct, pleasant or unpleasant, in the past, present, or future. Forms are classified according to whether they are causes or effects. There are four main types of causal form, and eleven main types that are effects.

Of the *four types of form which serve as causes,* the first is Earth in its most general sense as the ground for all activity. The second is Water, the cohering agent that brings things together. The third is Fire, whose basic characteristic is heat: it is the catalyst that makes things ripen. The fourth is Wind, which causes movement and dispersal.

There are *eleven types of resultant form.* The first five are the sense faculties, forms capable of perceiving sense objects. The second five are the sense objects themselves. The eleventh is a type of form of which I will speak in detail later.

Forms are further classified as being of two kinds: those with which contact can be made (by the hand, with a stick, and so on) and those which may be examined mentally (such as those which arise in meditation).

The first type of form is the faculty of the eye, which makes the eye able to perceive visual objects. It is compared to the *sarma,* a certain blue flower with a white center.

Then there is the form that is the faculty of the ear, the ability to hear. It is compared to the protuberances on the bark of a birch tree.

Next is the form which is the faculty of the nose, the sense of smell. It is like a cluster of fine copper needles which are hollow inside.

Then there is the form associated with the tongue, the faculty of taste. This is like a half-moon on the surface of the tongue.

Finally there is the kind of form that is the faculty of bodily feeling. It resembles the skin of the *rek na jam* [reg na 'jam], a bird in India which has fine down covering every part of its body.

The first of the *five sense objects* is form as object of the visual sense. Visual objects can be classified in two ways: by color and by shape. With regard to colors, four are basic: red, yellow, blue, and white. Included among color phenomena are dust, smoke, sunlight, shadow, and mist. All such appearances are modes of form as color. The shimmer that can be seen between the blue of the sky and the surface of the earth is also considered to be an example of this type of form. Even the sky itself, which has no shape, does nevertheless have a color, and is therefore also classified as form. Some colors are seen as pleasant, some as unpleasant, and some as neutral.

The other way of looking at visual form is with regard to shape—short, long, wide, thin, round, semi-circular, and so on. All the different shapes of inner and outer appearance we're familiar with are permutations of the category of form-as-shape. Some shapes are pleasant, some unpleasant, and some neutral.

The second type of sense object is sound, i.e., the objects perceived by the ear. Some sounds are made by sentient beings, human or animal, and can be vocal sounds or such sounds as finger snaps. Then there are sounds which do not arise from the activity of sentient beings, such as the sounds of earth, water, fire, wind, or rock. There are also sounds produced by the interaction of sentient beings and inanimate objects, such as the beating of a drum: the drum only produces a sound when struck by a being. Some sounds express meaning to sentient beings, others do not, such as the sounds of the elements. Amongst the sounds that express meaning are names and words used by worldly beings. There are also names and concepts used by Exalted Beings to express excellent and inconceivable meanings such as Body of the Buddha, Buddha Realm, and so on. In general, sounds can be pleasant, unpleasant, or neutral.

The third category of sense object is smell, in all its great variety. Scents can be pleasant, unpleasant, or neutral. Further, there are *inherent* smells, the natural smells of an object such as sandalwood, and *compounded* smells, such as that of incense.

Fourth are the tastes, the objects of the tongue. Six types are basic: sweet, sour, bitter, salty, pungent, and astringent. Through the mixture of these six arise many subclassifications. In general we can say that there are delicious tastes, bad tastes, and neutral tastes.

The fifth class of sense objects is the tactile, objects felt by the body. These can be categorized as causal feelings related to the four elements, and the seven resultant feelings: soft, rough, heavy, light, hunger, thirst, and cold. There are many other sorts of tactile sensations the body can experience, such as feelings of suppleness, tightness, relaxation, satisfaction, and feelings of illness, age, and death. A further distinction is made between tactile objects that are external to the body and those that are internal.

The eleventh class of form includes, firstly, *atomic form*, which, although it is matter can only be known by the mind but not seen. Then there is *imagined* form, such as reflected images and dreams. Then there is the kind of form seen through *the applied power of meditation*, in *samadhi*. There are also objects which are created through *the power of the mind alone*. At the stage of Buddhahood, one understands that in reality the four elements do not exist; therefore form that does not consist of the elements can be created, such as that in the Buddha Realms. Another instance of this eleventh type is a *form that can't be made known by appearance;* this is said to be involved in the taking of vows. From the time a vow is taken until the time it is broken or relinquished, a special type of form is involved. Imagine a monk who has taken vows but is not wearing any sort of monastic robes. Looking at him we don't know that he's a monk and has taken vows. But if his vows aren't broken, even though we can't see them, there still exists the imperceptible form of the vow, that which can't be made known by appearance.

Vows also include evil vows. If someone says, "I'll pay you a certain amount of money if you kill so-and-so," and you promise to commit the murder, you've taken a vow. Until you actually accomplish the deed, you're holding the vow.

The type of form which is generated by the taking of vows, whether good or evil, is inconceivably effective and extremely powerful. Even during sleep, or when the mind wanders and you seem to have forgotten about it, the vow still remains. But once the conscious decision is made not to keep the vow any more, and not to follow through with the plan, then the vow-form is destroyed. Therefore, being very careful about deeds of virtue and unvirtue is of great benefit, since such deeds are crucial to keeping vows. Basically, this vow-form is classified as form because its substance affects body and speech.

The collection of atoms of body and speech can also indirectly communicate knowledge to others. As a parallel: if pebbles are arranged to make the outline of a horse we don't see little stones, we see a horse, even though no horse is actually present, and we react accordingly. We see the horse rather than what communicates it. Because the form communicated is not the actual stones seen, this is another aspect of imperceptible form.

The ten types of form (the five sense faculties and their objects) can also be discussed in terms of their wide range of sizes. Working upward from the "most minute" particle, seven of which make one "minute" particle, and so on, we come to successively larger particles with names like "iron," "water," "rabbit," "sheep," "ox," "light ray" (equivalent to a dust mote in sunlight). Some larger units are "finger joint," 24 of which make one "cubit," four of which make one fathom ("bowspan"); 500 bowspans make one "earshot," eight of which make one *yojana*.

What we have discussed so far is related to the three realms of samsara (the Desire, Form, and Formless Realms). Within the Desire Realm there exist all five sense faculties and all five sense objects. However, in the realm of the higher gods there is no ear and no hearing, because the gods are able to perceive the analogues to sound without that particular sense. Thus, in the realm of the gods there are only eight types of form. As one progresses through the power of meditation into the Form and Formless realms, one finds fewer and fewer sense organs and sensory objects.

Q. How does matter disappear in the upper meditative realms?
A. When entering the meditative state, the sense of hearing first becomes inoperative, followed by the senses of smell, taste, bodily feeling, and finally the visual sense. The senses don't actually disappear: rather, you don't need to use them in meditation. A deeper sort of knowledge and understanding is available. The various senses are like crude tools; when meditative power has been developed, it provides more subtle and accurate types of information. Thus, the senses aren't actually lost, they just don't perform a function anymore.

Q. Why don't the gods hear sounds?

A. The only reason that one listens to sounds is to get cetain kinds of information. If you have that information through *samadhi*, you don't need to hear. This is the case for the gods.

Once when I was about fifteen years old in Tibet, I overheard my Root Lama Tarjay Gyamtso talking with the previous Jamgon Kongtrul Rinpoche. They were comparing notes about how they functioned. My Root Lama had the realization of a Buddha, and didn't need to use his senses. I was very young, of course, and didn't understand any of this. I thought it was very funny at the time. They were asking each other many questions such as, "Since you no longer have to perceive through your senses, if I held burning incense to your skin, would you feel it?" or "Will you be able to be aware of what I say without hearing it?" and that sort of thing. I laughed and couldn't understand that what they were speaking of resulted from the power of the mind in *samadhi*, arising through *shi nay*. Likewise, it is difficult for us to conceive how the gods, through the power of meditation, do or do not hear sounds, because we're not at that level. But it should be understood that the power of the mind always transcends the sense organs.

Q. When a person is dying, at what point does the sense of hearing disappear? If we're trying to give advice to a dying person who can no longer hear, how can we communicate—how does one reach such a person?

A. The elements of the five senses are very, very subtle and pure. They consist of earth, water, fire, and wind. During the process of dying, the connection between those elements, the external objects,and the mind is severed and you're no longer able to perceive through the sense organs. If you train in the teachings on bardo or on the Six Yogas of Naropa, you can slowly begin to understand this situation. The process of dying and the process of going to sleep are similar. Beacuse we are sentient beings, ignorance is very powerful while we sleep. If we haven't obtained teachings to transform this ignorance, the time of death will also be bewildering. In a dream you have the impression of being able to see and hear and smell, but your physical sense organs are not operative. You're not using the sense organs, but sense impressions arise through the power of habit.

In the dying process, there are three bardos. Between the *chi ka* and the *chö nyi* bardos, the senses "dissolve" back into the mind. After the *chö nyi* bardo is the *si pa* bardo, in which many sorts of experiences occur. This third bardo usually starts approximately three days after death, although this varies widely with different people. In any case, it is similar to falling asleep; one doesn't immediately start dreaming. There is an intermediate period before the appearances of the dream arise. If you are able to train well in the dream-state now, it will be easy for you at the time of death. You won't have much suffering then, or in the bardo, because you will understand the process. To train in the dream practice is not difficult. But for it to be successful, you need the blessings of your Lama, and to continue to accumulate merit and purify obscurations; then the whole process will be easy.

Q. With regard to the eleventh category of form, you said that the vow-form exists by manifesting through body and through speech. I'm wondering if this category applies only to vows, or if it also includes such things as beliefs and the patterns of our everyday behavior. Does it include the mental habits that alter or restrict our behavior?

A. Opinions and general beliefs are classified as part of the fourth skandha. Vow-form refers specifically to a certain kind of vow or decision to do something verbally or physically. When a vow is made, whether it be good or bad, the process resembles the transfer of an object from one person to another. For example, when you become a monk you must receive the vows from someone else who already holds those vows. The act of taking the vow also has very much to do with making a decision and determining that you are going to do something; there is always a specific purpose, an explicit intention. That distinguishes vows from other, more general kinds of beliefs that affect your actions.

This concludes our discussion of the first *skandha*, the aggregate of form. Now we will consider the Four Thoughts that Turn the Mind, which are the foundation of all Dharma teachings. We will begin by discussing the difficulty of finding the resources and opportunities of a precious human birth.

Meditation Practice

To fulfil what it means to have found a Precious Human Birth with its eight opportunities and ten resources it is essential to be aware of how rare the inconceivable power and ability we now have for practicing Dharma is. If we don't make use of this opportunity, we will soon lose it, and it will be difficult to find again.

All human beings can be classified as lesser, middling, or greater persons, with regard to basic motivation and ability. Lesser persons are those who practice virtue for the sake of improving their own situation during this lifetime in order to be happy and comfortable. The middling types are those who understand that this life is impermanent and full of suffering, and perform virtuous actions with the idea of achieving peace in the next lifetime. People of this second type have an understanding of cause and effect, and know that through negative behavior their next lives will be negative, while positive behavior will yield positive fruits later. The third, greater, type of person also understands the law of cause and effect, but in addition appreciates the fact that all sentient beings have been our parents. Such a person will not try to win peace just for himself or herself, but has the idea that it is necessary to purify karma and emotional afflictions so as to achieve perfect Buddhahood for the benefit of all beings.

With the precious human body, we are able to perform virtuous actions, cast off negative actions, practice the path of the Bodhisattva to attain Buddhahood as Milarepa did, and unfailingly accomplish in this life the benefit of all sentient beings. Therefore this precious human body that we've obtained is far more powerful than that of beings of the six realms such as the gods, nagas, and so on. When meditating on the difficulty of attaining the precious human existence, however, you must realize that its fruits will not necessarily appear in this lifetime but rather may not ripen until future lifetimes.

If the body were permanent and completely unchanging, any activity would be acceptable. Because the body really is impermanent, it is important to practice Dharma immediately. We cannot predict what kind of birth we will take in our next lifetime; we cannot assure ourselves that our next life will be happy or that we will avoid suffering. It is therefore important for us to think about the great sufferings of the three lower realms: the hell and hungry ghost realms that we cannot perceive; and the animal realm, of which we see only a part, and not even the part with the greatest suffering. When we consider very carefully the tremendous suffering of the lower realms, we rightly become sad and frightened.

On this topic there is a special meditation devised by Karma Chamay [chags med], a great Lama from eastern Tibet. He lived in the seventeenth century, during the time of the ninth and tenth Karmapas. I have received this teaching myself, and find it an especially effective method of meditation.

Begin by visualizing a high mountain. Around the mountain are regions full of beings of the six realms of samsara. Think about all the different kinds of karma that each of those sentient beings has, and all the various sufferings that each of them is experiencing. Reflect on them and visualize them very clearly. Then look at yourself: you have a sound body, can rely on Lamas, practice Dharma, and enter any path you choose. Reflect joyfully on the favorable situation you have attained and understand it to be the fruit of accumulated merit of virtuous actions in previous lives. Consider that all those sentient beings around the base of the mountain are experiencing the results of unvirtuous actions and are now suffering greatly. Then realize that your situation is also difficult — you too will fall into those realms of great suffering. At this point the thought comes to you that you must find some ultimate means of freeing yourself from this cycle of suffering.

Above and before you in the sky, visualize your Lama as any Yidam in the Buddhadharma in whom you have great faith. Meditate on him. For this particular practice, it is especially effective to visualize the Lama as Chenrezi, since this deity is known for his love and compassion. Imagine him as the essence of all Buddhas. Then hear the Lama say to you: "You have obtained a precious human body and are able to hear, contemplate, and practice the perfect Dharma. But if you don't accomplish virtuous action and abandon evil, no good will come. If you don't obtain an excellent human body in your next life, you will experience great suffering." Meditate on the suffering you will experience if you fall into each of the lower realms. This will encourage you to practice Dharma well.

By renouncing and accepting, your human life will be meaningfully fulfilled. Also think about the fact that all the sentient beings in the unending cycle of rebirths have at one time or another been your mother and very kind to you: therefore, arouse great compassion and feeling for their suffering. Resolve with determination that you will quickly establish each of them without exception in a Buddha realm.

Next, visualize that from Chenrezi's heart come rays of light. The rays touch you, purifying all the sins and obscurations of your body, speech, and mind. You are instantaneously reborn in Dewachen [bde ba can], the Pure Realm of Great Bliss. Then, through the power and ability you thus obtain, light rays emanate out from your heart and touch all sentient beings, purifying their suffering, sins, and obscurations; they too are reborn in the Pure Realm and become fortunate ones, completely enlightened. At this point, you can visualize yourself and all others as being Chenrezi.

Q. How does this meditation increase compassion?
A. It leads you to perceive the situation of all sentient beings, to understand that it is karma and emotional afflictions that have caused their great suffering. This in turn leads you to develop an extremely strong wish to remove beings from that state. You want to keep them away from suffering and give them happiness. Because this meditation was specifically devised by Karma Chamay Rinpoche to center on Chenrezi, the Bodhisattva of Loving Kindness, it increases the practitioner's compassion and love for sentient beings. The intention is to achieve a state of peace and bliss in the highest sense. The meditation on love, which is the act of wanting all sentient beings to have happiness, has as its result the attainment of peace. The meditation on compassion, which is the act of wanting to separate all sentient beings from any kind of suffering, has as its result the accomplishment of bliss.

Q. What if you have trouble visualizing? And for how long a period do you normally perform this meditation?
A. If you do not see this visualization clearly, you should not worry. It is actually very hard to visualize. In general, the best aid is the

strength of your resolution. You should generate intense determination that things be as the visualization describes.

However much time you spend on this practice is fine. But whether it is a long or a short period, the most important aim to be accomplished by the meditation is to develop compassion and love for sentient beings.

Sensation (tsor wa [tshor ba])

The second skandha is sensation. (This term can also be translated as feeling.) There are three basic types of bodily sensations: pleasurable, painful, and neutral. Mental sensations can be pleasurable or painful. The neutral mental sensation, or the feeling of equanimity, is not different from the neutral bodily sensation. In all, then, there are five types of sensation.

The six organs (eye, ear, nose, tongue, skin, mind) experience pleasurable, painful, and neutral sensations. Multiplying the six organs by the three sensations, we can list eighteen types of feeling. A simpler way of classification involves two categories: physical (the five senses) and mental feelings. Further, sensations may be divided with regard to whether they relate to material things, or if they involve cravings independent of material objects.

There are various intensities of sensation. Some are obvious and clearly felt, others are not. Suppose someone is sitting and writing, and there is another pen lying on the desk nearby. The writer is involved in his work, and when someone else comes and takes the other pen, he sees the pen being taken, but it doesn't register. But if later he is asked, "What happened to the pen?" he will suddenly realize that someone took it: the previous visual sensation is processed at this later time.

The reason that we describe this *skandha* or any of the five *skandhas* is so that you know what they are, and can recognize and understand the functions of mind. One should not try to eliminate them. The essence of sensation is impermanence. So the essence of happiness and suffering is impermanence. Not knowing this, we develop attachment. Clinging to their reality, our intentions become based on the hope for pleasurable sensation. Any feeling, good or bad, is impermanent. If the natural condition of sensation is really understood as impermanent, then attachment is somewhat relinquished. Because of this, the suffering of clinging to reality is lessened.

Recognition (du she ['du shes])

The third *skandha* is recognition. This is grasping at characteristics, which is synonymous with clinging to samsara as being real and permanent.

In the first instant of sensation, there isn't necessarily this grasping or attachment to the six senses (including the mind) and their corresponding objects. (The objects of the mind include images, memories, thoughts, and abstract concepts.) Sensation itself is a very direct, straightforward experience. It is in the second instant that there arises a grasping at the object. This grasping is the third *skandha*.

There are two aspects of this third *skandha*. The first is grasping at the attributes of objects; that is, the identification of an object, such as when one says, for example, "This is yellow. This is red. This is white." The second aspect is grasping of characteristics in conceptual terms. This involves differentiation of the object from other objects, as when one says, "This is a man. This is a woman." One can apprehend an object through its symbol, or, on the other hand, understand what an object is by its characteristics without even knowing its name.

Recognition is classified according to its scope. For example, if one's ability to recognize is limited to the six kinds of beings in the Desire Realm, it is considered to be small recognition. Those whose understanding can encompass the Form and Formless Realms within their sense fields are considered to have extensive recognition. Finally, there is immeasurable recognition, which starts with "infinitude of space" and extends all the way to the perception of a Buddha, which recognizes all the situations in the six realms without any limitation. The knowledge of a Buddha perceives every detail of every sentient being, including their thoughts and past lives.

Q. Would you explain the difference between the recognition of attributes, and the ability to differentiate between things, the faculty of making distinctions?

A. They are fundamentally the same. The difference is actually quantitative rather than qualitative. Recognition of objects is a very general ability to apprehend the nature of things. Apprehension through differentiation is a much subtler power, whereby one can apply different names to distinguish things within a particular category. If you are presented with a totally new object, you will see its color and shape, but you won't know what it is. You will also not be able to make a judgment about it. For example, if someone put an atom bomb in front of me, I would see it, but only as some sort of gray shape. I wouldn't necessarily know that it could kill us all.

Formation (du che [du byed])

The fourth *skandha* concerns what kind of activity is performed in the mind. In a general way, it refers to thoughts. In this *skandha*, there are fifty-one kinds of mental states or occurrences (sem chung [sems byung]); these states can be virtuous, unvirtuous, and so on.

The first group in the fifty-one consists of the five *omnipresent* mental occurrences. These are present no matter what type of activity the mind is engaged in. The first is *intention*, movement towards an object, as when one first thinks, "I will go, I will sleep, I will look, I will smell, I will conceive of an idea." Whatever sense faculties are involved, intention moves through one or more of these six senses.

The second is *concentration*, the mind one-pointedly grasping an image or concept. Next is *contact*, the connection of the mind to its object, which prevents other thoughts from disturbing the processing of cognition. The final two are the two *skandhas* described above, *sensation* and *recognition*. These five mental occurrences are all invariably present in any kind of thinking.

Next are the five mental states that are *determinative* with regard to the object: resolution, interest, recollection, *samadhi*, and wisdom. The first, *resolution*, performs the function of directing diligent efforts towards fulfilling any desired intention. In any virtuous or evil course of action, if you have a very powerful resolution, your diligence will be powerful too. The second determinative, *interest*, is holding to a particular thing or work to be done, and not allowing the mind to be "stolen" by anything else, even for a second. *Recollection*, the third determinative, prevents the mind from being distracted or forgetting the purpose at hand. *Samadhi*, the fourth, is the mind's one-pointed focus on something it is examining. Its function is to support knowing. *Wisdom*, the fifth determinative mental occurrence, is the opening up and complete development of the understanding of all examined phenomena.

The ten mental factors we've considered so far in the fourth skandha—the five which are omnipresent and the five which define and determine the object—are similar to one another, but each performs a different function. They may be difficult to distinguish, but if you investigate your own mind well, you can understand them even when they appear together simultaneously, as they do in certain kinds of mental activity. The difference between concentration and contact, for example, is between two aspects of a single stage of mind: one-pointed holding to an image or concept, and the non-arising of other thoughts. In one way all these ten are the same—as functions of the same mind. The five omnipresent occurrences are present in the same way in every mental act, while the five determinative mental occurrances will vary greatly in intensity depending on the power the object has in the mind. For example, whether in worldly work or in Dharma practice, if motivation and interest are powerful, then much can be accomplished. If they are weak, not much will be accomplished. If one's resolution is good, when one thinks "This is true, this is excellent," one will be able to bring it about. If one thinks one's objective is poor, then only difficulty will arise.

Eleven *virtuous* mental occurrences form another group within the fourth *skandha*. The first of these is *faith*, of which there are three types. One is the *faith of yearning*: you understand that in the lower realms of samsara and in any of the places of the six kinds of beings there is only suffering; thus you long for liberation, such as rebirth in a Buddha Realm like Dewachen. Through understanding that virtuous actions are a cause for happiness in the higher realms, and evil actions are a cause for suffering in the lower realms, you give rise to great trust in cause and effect, which is called *trusting faith.* When one understands that the Three Jewels are unfailing, and never a cause for suffering, and that they benefit many beings and are inconceivably excellent, then this is *clear faith.*

The next virtuous mental state is *carefulness*, where you understand that what one needs to cast off is evil action, and what one needs to take up is virtuous action. You apply care and mindfulness to practicing virtue and abandoning evil actions. All Lamas say that this is very important, and performs the function of enabling one to accomplish excellence in both existence and peace (i.e., samsara and Nirvana).

Another virtuous faculty is *thorough training.* It comes through training in *shi' nay* and enables one to use one's body and mind for virtue and to conquer negative influences.

Next is *equanimity*—you are not overpowered by emotional afflictions such as desire, hatred and stupidity, but instead remain in the natural state of the mind. When this peaceful mind is present, the emotional afflictions are not able to arise.

A *sense of propriety* is a virtuous aspect of mind that causes one to avoid committing a lot of unvirtuous actions. It involves understanding that certain actions are not good in terms of one's own standards or those of the Dharma. It serves as the basis for restraining faulty conduct through vows. Next, there is *considerateness*, which causes one to avoid actions that are judged unvirtuous by others or by worldly standards. This serves as the basis for remembering the kindness of one's parents or any other beings, and induces one to act in a similar fashion to others. These two, propriety and considerateness, work together and are very important. Propriety refers to yourself; it doesn't mean that you're ashamed of yourself, but rather that you're not the kind of person who does things without thinking of the effects. Through the factor of considerateness, you also become aware of what others will think of you, and you care very much for others.

Next is *non-attachment*, the mental attribute of extricating yourself from attachment to existence and samsaric things. It prevents one from getting involved with faulty conduct.

Lack of hatred is the state of being without animosity towards any sentient being or any condition that produces suffering. It causes one only to rejoice and not to enter into harmful conduct.

Lack of stupidity is understanding the meaning of things through discrimination, without dullness. Hence one is kept from mistakes or committing faults. Then there is *complete harmlessness*, which is compassion without any hatred. You do not conceive of others as enemies, so you don't want to harm them. Instead you have compassion for other beings, without any scorn. Finally, the eleventh virtuous mental occurrence is *diligence*, entering into virtuous activity with manifest delight. Through it, one can completely accomplish virtuous concerns.

Q. When the eighth virtuous mental occurrence, the lack of hatred, is present, and someone is actually doing you harm, do you just ignore them?
A. If you are attacked by an enemy, you need a means of keeping them from harming you. After the situation has ended, you shouldn't think, "This is my enemy." You should meditate on compassion and realize that the person was acting out of ignorance. You may know the Dharma, but that person does not, and so you should meditate with compassion, and not hold onto the thought, "This person is my enemy, and has done bad things to me." Now we will again leave the discussion of the five *skandhas*, and practice the meditation taught by Karma Chamay Rinpoche.

Meditation Practice

In the first meditation we considered the difficulty of obtaining a precious human existence. Now we will reflect on death and impermanence.

Usually our perceptions seem very real and permanent, whether they are of the container—the outside world—or its contents—sentient beings. Yet there is absolutely nothing in the phenomenal realm that is permanent. The external world is made up of the four elements. Even as science tells us, the elements that make up the container, the world, are constantly deteriorating year by year. They do not increase. If we have something like a house, at first it's in good shape, then it gets older and weaker every year. And generally speaking, because we are sentient beings, the internal contents of the world, we have more pain and sickness as we get older. Thus, both aspects of the world become worse and worse.

Nowadays, science and medicine, with all their new remedies and operations and examinations, are inconceivably more powerful than they were in previous times. Yet now there is also more and more suffering and sickness in the world, with many new diseases such as the different forms of cancer; in many ways life is cut short. In general, the situation of sentient beings is worsening, and less can be done to benefit them. If there were no impermanence, it would not be necessary to examine it. But since the force of impermanence will come to us all, it is beneficial to meditate on it. It is a profound method of practice. Year by year, month by month, we age, our suffering increases, and we approach death. Because of this, no activities will benefit us except Dharma. The only relevant principle that should concern us is that through performing virtuous deeds there is happiness, and by doing evil, there is suffering.

Q. Can an Enlightened being do anything about the suffering of the world?
A. Enlightened beings who have a tremendous store of merit can direct suffering to themselves and away from others. We aspire to this when we practice "Sending and Taking meditation" (tong len [gtong len]); a person of great merit can accomplish it actually and with great effect.

A long time ago Yeshe Tsogyal asked Guru Padmasambhava what could be done to help beings in the dark ages she foresaw. What could be done to alleviate their miseries in the time of the Kalpa of Great Conflict, the Kalpa of Weapons, and the Kalpa of Famine? Padmasambhava answered: "In order to help eliminate intense sufferings in that dark time, make supplications to one who is now one of my twenty-five foremost disciples, and who in the future will bear the name Karmapa. Sincere supplications and devotion to that being will bring about harmony."

In 1981 I was present during the Gyalwa Karmapa's last illness, and I believe that what I saw then was a fulfillment of Guru Rinpoche's prophecy. By the time I saw him, His Holiness had already had many operations, some parts of his body removed, things put inside him, his blood tranfused, and so on. Every day the doctors discovered the symptoms of some new disease, only to find them gone the next day and replaced by another illness, as if all the diseases in the world were finding room in his flesh. For two months he had taken no solid food, and finally his doctors gave up hope. It was impossible for him to live, and the doctors thought the life-support systems should be disconnected.

But the Karmapa said, "No, I'm going to live. Leave them in place." And he did live, astonishing the doctors, and remaining seemingly at ease in his situation—humorous, playful, smiling, as if he were rejoicing at everything his body suffered. Then I thought, with the clearest possible conviction, that the Karmapa had submitted to all this cutting, to the manifestation of all those diseases in his body, to the lack of food, in a quite intentional and voluntary way: he was deliberately suffering all of these diseases to help minimize the coming pains of war, disease, and famine, and in this way he was deliberately working to avert those terrible kalpas. For those of us present, his death was an unforgettable inspiration. It profoundly revealed the efficacy of the Dharma, and the fact that Enlightenment for the sake of others can actually be achieved.

Karma Chamay has given us an excellent way of meditating on death and impermanence. First, you enter again into the realm of the imagination. Visualize that you're alone on a vast plain, empty of all other beings. There are very high mountains, and there is the sound of water. Below the plain in a valley is a large river filled with sentient beings.

Next, the sun sets and it becomes very dark. You are frightened. Since you are in an unfamiliar place, you do not know where you are as you walk around in the dark. You become even more afraid. Suddenly you find yourself at the edge of a cliff, and in danger of falling into the river in the gorge below. You grasp at two clumps of grass with your two hands, which keep you from falling into the abyss. As you hang there in great fear, there appears at your right a little white mouse, and on the left a little black mouse that come out from the rocks. The white mouse begins to chew on the bunch of grass your right hand clutches, while the black mouse chews the bunch of grass your left hand holds. The clumps are becoming thinner and thinner. You are in a state of panic because you know that any second now you could fall into the river and drown. And you know the river is full of various creatures that could eat you.

At this point you will realize how negligent you have been in the practice of Dharma. Then you see Lama Chenrezi in the sky, and you make many prayers to him. Lama Chenrezi says, "Whoever is a sentient being has sickness, death, and suffering. The nature of everything is impermanence. When you attain freedom you will practice well. Pray to your Lama." Then with faith, longing, and determination you pray intensely to Lama Chenrezi. At the moment the two mice finish the last blade of grass, light rays emanate from the heart of Lama Chenrezi and strike one's heart, purifying the obscurations of body, speech and mind. You are instantly reborn as Chenrezi in the pure land of Dewachen. Meditate with love and compassion. Inconveivable numbers of light rays emanate from your heart, touch all the beings of the six kinds, purify their sufferings, evils and obscurations, and guide them to Dewachen.

This meditation could be elaborated upon in many ways. The most important point is what benefits your mind. You should observe the results of the meditation and ascertain which sections of the sequence seem useful for your individual needs. You can emphasize and spend more time on any one part. In particular, if you are a person with great pride, hatred, etc., and find it difficult to practice Dharma, this meditation is very beneficial.

Formation: The Fourth Skandha *Continued*

Of the fifty-one formations, we have already discussed the first twenty-one, which included the five omnipresent ones, the five that determine the object, and the eleven virtuous ones.

Now we will consider the twenty-six *unvirtuous* mental occurrences. There are six root emotional afflictions and twenty subsidiary emotional afflictions.

Of the six *root afflictions* only five are emotional afflictions, while the sixth, *view*, which is divided into five parts, is placed in this category for the purpose of Dharma explanation.

The root of all emotional affliction is *ignorance.* Ignorance here means not knowing about action and result, the true meaning and way of practice according to the Precious Jewels. Not understanding these things is the source or foundation of all emotional afflictions. Ignorance itself is unable to perform any function. It obscures the understanding of actions and their results—that virtue leads to happiness and evil leads to suffering; it obscures the understanding of the Four Noble Truths, of Relative and of Ultimate Truth, and the excellent qualities of the Three Jewels. It obscures the understanding of impermanence and change. Because of all this, all the other afflictions come into being.

The second of the emotional afflictions is *desire*, which is the grasping at the deteriorating aggregates of the three realms. It produces the suffering of existence and causes all the sentient beings of the six types to circle in samsara. It arises from the obscuration of ignorance.

There are two types of desire. One is *desire of desire*, a desire for actual things among the three realms of samsara; it pertains to beings of the six types in the Desire Realm. In the two upper realms, the Form Realm and the Formless Realm, there isn't this manifest desire, but there is the *desire for existence*. The higher god-states such as infinite space, infinite consciousness, etc., are the fruit of great merit obtained through *samadhi*-meditation. But because the grasping at an "I" has not been abandoned, those gods have not turned away from samsaric existence.

Thirdly, there's the emotional affliction of *anger*. Anger is the relentless desire to hurt other beings. It's impossible to be happy while you're angry, and so we consider it to be the origin of unhappiness.

The fourth basic emotional affliction is *pride*, an attitude of inflated superiority supported by worldly views. It is thinking, "I'm great," "I'm a high person," "I have great qualities," "I have an excellent form." There are said to be seven kinds of pride. It prevents you from respecting others and causes you to be unhappy.

The fifth is *doubt*. It is being of two minds concerning the true meaning. You are not certain whether the Dharma is really true or not. You think, "This isn't true," "this isn't good." Ignorance is very strong and trust impossible. You become unable to practice virtue and usually are drawn towards negative action.

The sixth is *view*. Here we mean negative views based on the emotional afflictions. There are views without any emotional affliction, which are considered "Perfect View." But the views we are discussing are all considered "wrong view."

There are five types of view. The first is the *view based on the perishable aggregates*, the strong belief that in the five *skandhas* there is actually a self. This view becomes the basis for all wrong views.

Second is the *view that holds to extremes*; this is the view that the self or the *skandhas* exist permanently (eternalism) or that they don't exist at all (nihilism). Both views block the arising of certainty in the Middle Path—the Ultimate View.

The third is the *inverted view,* which denies that which is real such as the truth of karma, cause and effect, and the Three Jewels. Whoever has this view is not inclined towards virtuous activity.

That completes the three negative views. Then there are the two forms of "holding as supreme"—*holding these views as supreme* and *holding conduct based on them as supreme.* The first of these, the fourth of the wrong views, is the attitude that your erroneous view is the very best. In this case, you are completely convinced that a view such as the denial of karma is true, good, perfect, and you don't look at any other view. Since all that concerns body and speech is a projection of mind, you always need to examine with awareness the validity of your view and not accept it dumbly.

The second of these is *holding one's morality and conduct as supreme.* This means holding to conduct and morality that is not conducive to liberation. This kind of view is not beneficial for oneself or others. Still one holds it as being the very best and all other moral disciplines as being untrue and bad.

Because these two—holding one's view as supreme and holding one's morality and conduct as supreme—involve clinging to the five *skandhas,* they are like a rope that binds you tightly. All activity is exhausting and fruitless. Even if an activity is engaged in with a lot of energy, it is meaningless. These five views are not a means of liberation from samsara and therefore not a real path.

According to the teachings of the Buddha, to determine whether a view is true or not, real or not, you need to examine your own mind. An individual must accomplish liberation in the Dharma by himself. Therefore, you must always decide for yourself whether a view leads to liberation or not. When it does, then you will also understand what is really beneficial for oneself and others now as well as in the future. In short, you always have to use your own intelligence to investigate these things for yourself. If you don't constantly do this, and instead merely cling to a view, you can never attain freedom from samsara.

Fundamentally, the teaching of the Buddha is to practice virtue and abandon evil. By using your own intelligence to examine what is right and what is wrong, and to develop this understanding through experience, produces the faith of trust.

We have obtained a human body. Because of this, a teacher—a Lama, Friend of Virtue—is needed to explain the mind in words you can understand—human terms—and to guide you. But you always have to decide yourself whether what the teacher says is true, and whether it really works or not: if it is going to be of benefit, who it will benefit, how it will benefit, and when it will benefit. You must always examine such questions, because if you just listen to the teacher and agree automatically just because it is his word, then you're no different from an animal. You have to use your intelligence to understand the truth.

Once you really understand the meaning and nature of things well, and have reached a decision as to what is true, you should feel confidence in it. There is no need for doubt and a lot of additional activity.

When you're involved in Dharma practice or Dharma work it is not an instantaneous process, where you do something and get an immediate result. You have to look at the situation in its entirety: what work was done before and what kind of fruit has come, what kind or result comes from perfecting oneself. For example, in the case of Milarepa, a great Tibetan Siddha, and many others like him, we have to consider what work was done previously, what work was done in between, what experiences occurred, what benefit for other beings there was, and what the situation at the time of death was. Dharma practice must be considered from a very broad perspective. Therefore, examining the characteristics of views is very important.

Finally, there are several ways of distinguishing types of views: one is *innate*, naturally present, such as the view of the perishable aggregates based on the self and the five *skandhas*; the other is *acquired* through investigation or instruction by a teacher such as the two kinds of Holding as Supreme. Actions based on acquired views are easily abandoned, but actions based on innate views are much more difficult to let go of. According to the Buddha's teaching, the one hundred and fourteen acquired views are abandoned through understanding the meaning of things and developing certainty. The three hundred and sixty innate views only meditation can dispel.

Q. What is an example of an innate view?

A. It's the view of clinging to a self — the view of the perishable aggregates. Clinging to an "I" in the five *skandhas*, you think, "I'm sick," "I'm in pain," "I'm unhappy," "I'm happy." Or "I feel," "I perceive," "I think." These views are always grounded in clinging to an "I" in what is only the five skandhas.

An example of an acquired view would be the different doctrines of eternalism and nihilism that are learned or based on deduction or inference. Thus, if you have the belief that each person was created by someone, then you will believe that someone must have created the Buddha, even though there is no evidence for that view. That would be an example of an acquired view.

Of the five emotional afflictions, the three major ones, ignorance, desire, and hatred, are all inherent. The other two, pride and doubt, are acquired. For example, pride may arise from hearing yourself praised: "You're great," "You have excellent qualities," "You're beautiful." One comes to acquire this view of oneself, too. Likewise, being taught that something isn't true could be cause for acquiring doubts. Holding your own views as supreme is also an acquired view.

Q. You said that the main injunction of the Buddha's teachings is to test and re-test our views with our own intellect, and that blind faith is to be avoided. Now on some levels of the path, especially the Vajrayana, it is not possible for beginners to fathom the answer to all their questions. Faith is said to be extremely important and the root of accomplishment here. Could you say something about this sort of faith?

A. Whichever vehicle you're practicing, the Hinayana, Mahayana, or Vajrayana, there is no difference — you need the faculty of examination. The Buddha said, "My teaching is like gold: melt it, pound it, cut it — it is always excellent." So the teaching of the Buddha can be examined as much as you want, and it will still be true. Thus all the vehicles are the same in that examining their meaning it will only develop your understanding; as a result, your certainty will allow you to work one-pointedly. The Vajrayana is no different. You need to examine: how does one train on this path? what is the fruit of this?

On the Vajrayana path, you must also evaluate the teacher. When the Lama explains the Dharma, does it benefit you? Does it benefit sentient beings? Just because it is the Vajrayana Dharma, you can't just think: "It's the Vajrayana!" and set aside any examination. You have to determine whether the Lama has abandoned personal gain and is presenting the teaching for the benefit of all sentient beings, leading them on the path to liberation from suffering, and towards Buddhahood. One must examine this carefully; just assuming that because it's the Vajrayana one can't examine the teacher is the wrong attitude. Proper examination is very important. Trust results from it. Certainly you can investigate the great Lamas, like Kalu Rinpoche, Dezhung Rinpoche,* Ling Rinpoche,† and Dudjom Rinpoche,‡ great teachers of all the four schools, and find that they are indeed worthy Lamas. So, even in the Vajrayana, there is no such thing as faith without examination.

If you discover that a teacher is not satisfactory you are always free to leave and find one who can benefit your practice. There are many Lamas who can do so. Once you have investigated and found the Lama to be qualified, then you should put your faith in him. And after you have received profound instructions from a teacher, you can't disparage him. You have established an important connection with him, and to criticize him at that point would be a negative act that will destroy your Dharma practice.

Q. Is it possible that some people do not make any examination whatsoever, yet happen to hold the right point of view? Can you hold blindly and uncritically to the real truth?
A. It is not possible to have attachment to the perfect view, since someone who has the perfect view must have real understanding and experience. Once you have them, there naturally can be no attachment or mental blindness.

It is said, "If there is grasping, then it is not "perfect view." This comes from the famous *Shenpa Shidrel* [zhen pa bzhi 'bral], a teaching of the Sakyapas consisting of four verses:

> If you are attached to this life,
> You are not a Dharma person.

---

*A contemporary master of the Sakya lineage, who has taught for many years at the University of Washington.
†Late head of the Gelügpa Lineage and senior tutor to the Dalai Lama.
‡Chief representative of the Nyingmapa lineage, with numerous Dharma centers in the West.

If you are attached to samsara,
You don't have renunciation.

If you are attached to your own benefit,
You don't have Bodhicitta.

If there is grasping,
You don't have the view.

Q. Does the term "middle path" refer to avoiding the extreme views of nihilism and eternalism? What exactly is it?
A. The middle path (Madhyamaka) rejects both extremes, both the view that says, "Yes, something is," and the view that says, "No, something is not." You can't definitely assert that something is, because ultimately nothing is seen by the Buddhas. You also can't assert that nothing exists, because the mind is the basis for samsara, the lower realms, and so on. The Middle view is not a synthesis of these opposites, however, because it transcends existence and non-existence.

The basis of the middle path is interdependence — the union of the two truths, the relative and absolute. The path itself is the perfection of merit, which deteriorates, and primordial knowledge, which does not deteriorate. The fruit is the union of the two Kayas — the Rupakaya and the Dharmakaya. The Dharmakaya is the realization of the mind's essence, and benefits oneself. It is the attainment of the ultimate truth. The Dharmakaya doesn't benefit sentient beings directly. Through its power come the two aspects of the Rupakaya: the Samboghakaya and the Nirmanakaya, like light rays from the sun, which function to benefit sentient beings. The Rupakaya is the attainment of the relative truth.

Q. About testing the truth for oneself — some truths, like that of cause and effect (karma) don't manifest fully in one lifetime. They can't really be tested except over a period of several lifetimes. Some karma does manifest itself in one lifetime, when the fruits of a good or bad deed take effect, yet many other situations need several lifetimes to come to fruition. How can you test the truth of karma if you can't remember your past lives?
A. Because of the obscuring power of ignorance, it is difficult to understand and trust the full workings of cause and effect. But the truth of the karmic process can be demonstrated in a general way

through examples and their implications, even though it is not always possible to actually see the precise effects of everything that you do. For example, a mother and father might have five children, each very different from the others. Their ideas are different, their activity is different, their physical characteristics are different, and their situations are completely different. The immediate circumstances, their manner of birth, their environment are clearly the same for each of the children. Yet their lives are different. Likewise, in the world there are all sorts of variations in health, longevity, happiness, and so on. All such variations are attributable to karma. If you continually examine the way things occur you will understand something of cause and effect. A day or two is not enough to see results. This is because the obscuration of ignorance is very powerful.

The Buddha said, "To understand your previous actions look at your present life; to understand your future life look at your present actions." If you practice virtue, it will have a good result; if you do evil, the result will be correspondingly negative. To believe precisely and totally in this law is very difficult. We gain conviction through examples and reasoning, but to see the process in detail is difficult. Only a Buddha can know exactly the nature of every single cause and every single result.

In this life if you train in school from the time you're young, you can obtain a good job later on. If you train well at anything the results are good. Likewise one can infer that if the present life is used well, the future lives will be good, although it may be difficult to see. If one's intentions are good and one wishes to benefit others, then this will be a cause for virtuous karma. If intentions are bad, then they'll be a negative cause.

The Buddha said, "Our own intentions are the best way to be kind to ourselves." Through our good thoughts and positive actions towards others, our own situation continues to improve lifetime after lifetime until we reach Buddhahood.

Q. When you listed the five emotional afflictions the fifth one was doubt. Isn't the fifth one usually jealousy?
A. In this particular system the fifth obscuration is doubt. In other systems, jealousy is listed here. Jealousy is not a root affliction, but a

subsidiary one. Jealousy is dependent upon hatred, desire and pride, and is therefore a "branch" emotion, whereas doubt, although related to stupidity, is a "principal" one.

The first of the twenty *subsidiary* emotional afflictions is *wrath*, which is internal anger that has increased over time and readies one actually to harm other beings through actions such as beating.

The second, *malice*, is a variety of internal anger. In this case the intention to harm someone has become very powerful and continuous. You can't let go of it and it makes you unforgiving.

The third is *rage*. When the causes of both wrath and malice become unbearable, you show it — your face turns red and you speak harsh, angry words.

Then, fourth is *vindictiveness*, another kind of internal anger that is not expressed. It is the absence of love and compassion. Outwardly you might appear gentle but inside you seek revenge. Vindictiveness causes one to despise others.

The fifth is *jealousy*. Jealousy is also classified as a kind of internal anger. It is caused by attachment to acquisitions and honor. You can't bear for others to have good things or qualities. Jealousy agitates your mind greatly and, being so unhappy, you can never let it rest. Jealousy arouses anger and causes you to lose much of the merit that may have been gained previously.

Then, sixth, there is *deceitfulness*. Being attached to acquisitions and honor, you hide your faults. Constantly doing this, you are engaged in a lot of crookedness. This is classified as a combination of desire, anger, and stupidity. It becomes an obstacle to receiving instructions from a teacher.

Seventh is *hypocrisy*. In order to gain possessions or respect you pretend to have qualities you don't have. Because those qualities are not factual, you are involved in deceiving others. This is classified as attachment and ignorance, and causes you to practice wrong livelihood.

The eighth affliction is *shamelessness*. This is complete lack of propriety. Here, one's standards do not include the avoidance of evil actions. Shamelessness is classified as a combination of the three poisons and accompanies all root and branch emotional afflictions.

The ninth is *inconsiderateness*. With regard to others you do not avoid evil actions. It is also manifest as ingratitude for the good things others have done for you, such as your parents or Lama. While shamelessness relates to yourself, inconsiderateness relates to others. It's also classified as a combination of the three poisons and accompanies all the afflictions.

Then there is *concealment*. This is covering up your faults to avoid being admonished by others to behave well. It is classified as a mixture of attachment and stupidity, and causes one to feel no remorse.

The next affliction is *greed*. It is caused by desire. Greed is intense clinging to possessions, and causes one continually to want to increase them. As the Buddha said, "Where there is great power there is great evil, where there is great wealth there is great greed."

The twelfth of the subsidiary afflictions is *vanity*, a kind of pride. It is being attached to and delighted with one's good health, beauty, youth, good qualities, etc. It is like being intoxicated with oneself.

Then there is the thirteenth, *lack of faith*. This is a kind of stupidity that causes one to have no interest in perfect objects—the practice of virtue and Dharma—and therefore one accomplishes nothing for oneself or others.

The fourteenth is *laziness*. Being attached to the pleasure of negative actions, you take no joy in the practice of virtue and think, "It's too difficult for my body and health." Because this runs contrary to diligence, you accomplish nothing.

Carelessness comes from the three poisons and laziness. You lose the ability to distinguish between what is good and bad, and therefore cannot take up virtuous actions and abandon evil ones. This lack of concern runs contrary to carefulness.

The next of the afflictions is *forgetfulness*: you cannot remember clearly virtuous objects. You come wholly under the influence of the other emotions, and the mind becomes distracted. This kind of forgetfulness principally occurs during Dharma practice, for example, when you're going for Refuge or engendering Bodhicitta and are not able to concentrate your mind on what you're doing, or even the meaning of it.

Seventeenth is *lack of conscience.* This is said to be a "distracted wisdom" because even though you realize what are the right things to do and even understand why they are right, your emotional afflictions prevent you from doing those things. You can't conduct your body, speech, and mind the way you want to when the time comes to do so. It causes moral failings.

Then there is the affliction called *fogginess,* which is actually a form of ignorance. It is a state in which the body and mind feel very heavy and you are not able to visualize clearly or to concentrate. It makes you vulnerable to the various emotional afflictions.

There is also *wildness* that results from desire. You desire certain things, and your mind runs after them; you're not able to stay in a state of serenity. It is a very strong tendency that is an obstacle to *shi nay* meditation.

Finally, there is *distraction.* It is classified as consisting of all three poisons. Here, the mind is constantly wandering in different directions and can't stay on any virtuous object. There are many different kinds of distraction that are distinguished — internal, external and so forth.

Q. Sometimes we speak simply of good and bad deeds, while at other times we hear that dualism is a wrong view. How does one reconcile this apparent contradiction?
A. If dualistic distinctions are made with a clear understanding of the law of interdependent origination, they can be useful, as when we differentiate good and bad on the relative level. It is essential, however, to ground these distinctions in the truth of emptiness. Once you lose your basic understanding of relativity and begin to hold the distinctions as real, you've fallen into a wrong view.

Q. If negative states of mind seem to become stronger in the course of our practice, and even become overwhelming, is that the result of an error in practice, or is it a sign that the practice is taking effect?
A. The practice of meditation is difficult. There are many things that occur in the mind. Sometimes negative aspects of mind seem to increase. This is simply a sign that your negativity is becoming clear to you. Tremendous upheaval occurs in the mind when you begin to meditate, and propensities that were previously latent become

manifest. This doesn't mean that those propensities are increasing, but rather that you are becoming more aware of them.

Meditation Practice

Now we'll leave the discussion of the skandhas for a while and return to the meditation instructions given in the teachings of Karma Chamay Rinpoche.

His third meditation is on the law of cause and effect; it is particularly relevant to our discussion of the virtuous and unvirtuous occurrences of mind. His method is traced to the Indian Siddha Shawaripa, one of the eighty-four Mahasiddhas.

Imagine that in front of you is a huge mirror, like a vast television screen. In this mirror you can see distinctly the six realms of samsara. Think about the fact that after you die and enter the bardo of Becoming, the force of your previous actions will determine the realm in which you must take rebirth.

Next, visualize Yama, the great Dharma King, on a large throne. Here Dharma refers particularly to laws—rules of conduct. Into his presence is brought someone who has committed many evil acts. From the right and left sides of Yama appear two people who are personifications of karma. One is white, the other black. The white figure speaks on behalf of the defendant, recalling all the virtuous things he or she has done: Dharma practice, and so forth. The black figure speaks to accuse the defendant of evil actions. The two argue like lawyers before a judge in a courtroom.

Meanwhile, Yama and the jury are scrutinizing a mirror which shows the actual truth of what the defendant has done in the past; they read a record of all previous deeds. They weigh these on a scale to determine which is heavier, virtue or evil.

Since the jury has authoritative records and can judge clearly, it's not possible to lie or to cover up the defendant's faults. And so the jury decides that this person has committed grave misdeeds and will now have to go to the deepest hell.

Next a second defendant, a good person, is brought before Yama. Again the evidence is presented: the jury looks into the mirror, reads the records, weighs all the deeds; and again, there is no lying or concealing. In this case, when all the evidence has been considered, even though there has been arguing on both sides, it seems clear that this person who has done virtuous actions is going to be reborn in the higher realms.

If one has a record of virtuous actions, a peaceful disposition, and accomplishment in developing the mind, no accuser can prove the person to be evil. Such a person cannot suffer the ill effects or obscurations that result from wrong deeds. All these appearances in the bardo are only manifestations of previous activity.

Meditate on these two scenes and apply them to yourself. How would you fare in such a situation? Contemplate the results of virtuous and evil deeds. Consider the fact that in this situation there is no posssibility of lying about any evil actions you have ever done. There is no one you can ask to help you at this point. Meditate on the certainty of the ripening of your karmic seeds and the inevitable appearance of their fruits. Resolve that when you meet the Dharma King, you won't be in the position of having to be ashamed of previous evil actions. If your activity in this life is virtuous, at the time of death there won't be any need to be ashamed or afraid, because you won't have any feeling of guilt.

This is a meditation from Shawaripa on the events that will occur during the bardo of Becoming.

In Tibet, knowing about this was easy. Among us there were certain unusual people, such as one woman who was famous in my country. After being dead for about seven days, such people could, if nothing had been done to the corpse, come back to life. During those seven days these individuals might see the states of existence, the pure realms, and also the bardo, where they might witness the fates of many people. When they return to life they are able to relate what they have seen. These people are not like Western psychics; this is a somewhat different phenomenon — it's actual experience. Such people have related their experiences to great Lamas such as the Gyalwa Karmapa or Dudjom Rinpoche, and these Lamas have confirmed that their stories were authentic.

I have met one of them, and I can tell the difference between some foolish people I've met in America who claim all sorts of things, and someone who has actually had this kind of experience. You must practice much virtuous activity to be this sort of individual. The person I knew was the mother of Tarjay Gyamtso, my root Lama. When my teacher was young, he knew a man who wasn't really much of a practitioner but had posed as a great Lama. My teacher asked his mother how this man had fared after death, in the bardo. My teacher's mother answered, "Oh, him? He wasn't a real Lama, was he? He wasn't a real monk, nor was he even an ethical and virtuous person. Right now, he's trying to communicate with his relatives, telling them that they should do good deeds so that they can avoid the trouble he is having." In another case she told my teacher about a great Lama of that region, truly a great monk and practitioner, who died and had reached the Pure Realm of Sangdok Palri [zangs mdog dpal ri]. Both of these people in life had seemed to be Dharma people, but when they died the truth was known. When my teacher's mother herself died, her teacher, a great Lama named Garchen Tulku, performed the ritual of transference for her. Through the excellence of her intention and the power of this Lama, she was reborn in the eastern part of the country as a young boy who later became a monk.

In general, the result of practicing the Dharma is that one's future lives do not become worse, but naturally improve in accordance with one's practice.

Formation: The Fourth Skandha Continued

Now we return to the fifty-one formations constituting the fourth *skandha*. We have discussed the five omnipresent ones, the five that determine the object, the eleven virtuous ones, the six root emotional afflictions, and the twenty subsidiary emotional afflictions: altogether, forty-seven have been considered.

The remaining four are the four *variable* states, which can be virtuous or unvirtuous. First is *sleep*, classified as stupidity, where all the sense fields are drawn inside. Whether it is meritorious or non-meritorious is determined by your state of mind as you are falling asleep. This can affect the dreams that follow. If one has trained well in virtue, then these tendencies will appear in the dream state. Similarly, if one mostly indulges in the emotional afflictions, one's dreams will reflect this.

Second is *remorse*. This is unhappiness about what you've done before. Because it breaks your concentration, it is an obstacle to resting the mind. However, remorse is an element of confession. In order for confession to be an effective means of purifying unvirtuous activity, there must be remorse for previous actions. Here it functions as a virtuous tendency.

Third is *investigation*. Relying on intention and wisdom, it is the mind's descriptive process as it seeks an object. When form is distant in the range of the senses, you are able to determine the identity of it roughly. Seeing a sentient being at a great distance you speculate, "It's a cow," "It's a horse," but you can't distinguish.

Finally, there is *examination*. Depending on intention and wisdom, you are able to discriminate the differences in a particular object. It is a fine mental analysis. For example you would not only understand an object to be a vase, but also that it was new, without cracks, etc.

Because these four are dependent upon whether the specific thoughts or conceptions involved are themselves virtuous, unvirtuous or neutral, they are called the Four Variables.

This completes our discussion of the fifty-one mental states of the fourth *skandha*.

Consciousness (nam shay [rnam shes])

The fifth *skandha*, consciousness, has as its characteristics clarity and knowing. Consciousness is divided into six types corresponding to the six sense faculties. Thus there is eye consciousness, nose consciousness, ear consciousness, tongue consciousness, body consciousness, and mind consciousness. Here we conceive of the mind as a sense faculty because it can recall past events and perceive various mental objects. Through all six types of consciousness, one can know distinctly the nature and characteristics of phenomena.

With the support of the sense faculty, the corresponding intelligence arises. In the first instant of contact the faculty apprehends the object, yet the faculty itself is not capable of knowing its object. That is the function of consciousness: to hold onto the object in the second instant of contact that occurs. Without the faculty there can be no consciousness. But it is consciousness that does the actual work. That is why it is called, for example, "eye-consciousness." By eye-consciousness we mean that basic intelligence which knows an object perceived by the eye. Each consciousness responds only to the corresponding faculty and object. It is not an unimpeded process. For example, when eye-consciousness knows its object in that second instant, ear consciousness is blocked, and so on. After the first moment of contact between a sound and the ear, the ear-consciousness knows about the perceptions of the sound, whether it is good or bad, whatever, in the second moment. When by means of the nose, contact takes place with an odor, basic intelligence takes hold of the object and knows it in the second moment; that is olfactory consciousness. Similarly, after contact between the tongue and a tasteable object, consciousness in the next moment will hold and know the event. So also with the body: after there is contact with the body, consciousness can know in the second moment whether the sensation was pleasant or unpleasant, and so on. Finally, after the mind faculty perceives a mental phenomenon, basic intelligence is able to take hold and understand it. It can know any situation in the mind—happiness, suffering, and so on.

In the Hinayana tradition, just these six consciousnesses are counted. According to the sutras and commentaries of the Mind-Only school of the Mahayana, there are eight types of consciousness. Supported by Basic Consciousness, confused mind posits the View of a Self, Pride (thinking "I"), Attachent to a Self, and Ignorance. The mind with these four emotional afflictions is known as the "Emotionally afflicted mind" and is the *seventh consciousness*. Except for those who have actualized the stages of a Bodhisattva or the Truth of Cessation or the Path of No More Learning, all beings have this kind of consciousness.

Finally, the *eighth consciousness* is the Basic Consciousness (kun shi nam she [kun gzhi rnam shes]). It is called this because it is the basis, the ground that holds the seeds—the *skandhas, ayatanas, dhatus*, and so forth. In clear awareness, the basis of the mind, occur all the places in the six realms, external objects, the bodies we inhabit in each. All the karmic seeds for taking birth in these realms are held by Basic Consciousness and so it is called the "taking consciousness." All these different places, bodies, and objects are like appearances in a dream, or images in a mirror. Although they are "mere appearance," without any ultimate reality, they are planted through habit and sustained by Basic Consciousness. Thus it is also called the "ripening consciousness."

By and large, the different terms *sem* [sems], *yi* [yid] and *nam she* [rnam shes] have the same referent. But more specifically, *sem* connotes the basic consciousness and *yi* the emotionally afflicted consciousness, while *nam she* refers to the collection of the six consciousnesses.

This concludes our discussion of the five *skandhas*, under which are subsumed all composite phenomena. The reason for studying the five *skandhas* is to destroy our powerful attachment to a self in these *skandhas*. We tend to identify one or another of the five *skandhas* as what we are—"my physical form," "my sensations," and so on. To help eradicate this, all the constituents of the *skandhas* are enumerated. In the Mahayana path of training one works to eliminate clinging to the body, speech and mind. Although we think, "This is my body, my speech, my mind," it is not so: such thoughts are only obscurations. Understanding this, one examines also the emotional afflictions and the workings of all fifty-one mental occurrences. Here one actually observes the mind to see what sort of virtuous thoughts and what sort of unvirtuous thoughts occur. Because an understanding of the workings of consciousness is crucial for the practice of meditation, it is important to learn the terminology of the *skandhas*.

In the Vajrayana, the path of method, there is a further development of the concept of the five *skandhas*, namely, their transformation. Here, once you have understood the *skandhas*, you can begin to consider how those factors can appear in either impure form or pure form. Since this is the path of method, one's concern is how to transform them. If you can recognize the five *skandhas*, it makes transformation easier. The impure *skandhas* become equivalent in their pure aspect to the Buddhas of the Five Families. But it is important to understand what the five *skandhas* are and how they really work, in order to see how they can manifest as the Five Buddhas. For example, some of the ornaments worn by the deities correspond to the fifty-one formations. If you don't know what these formations are, you cannot understand what the pure symbols adorning yidams and Buddhas represent. Thus by investigating the five *skandhas*, one's understanding of Dharma, epecially the Secret Mantrayana, will gradually improve.

Q. You said that one of the values of the teaching on the *skandhas* is to eliminate the view that there is a self. It seems to me that the

Mind Only view which posits an eighth consciousness as the basis of all the different aspects of mind, karma and its effects, is moving back towards an affirmation of some kind of concrete individual.

A. What we have been talking about is the functioning of the mind of a sentient being. When the person becomes enlightened and becomes a Buddha, the distinction between the Mind only school and the Madhyamaka school dissolves, since the Basic Consciousness (the eight consciousness) is transformed into the Dharmakaya. With regard to unliberated consciousness, there seems to be a slight difference between the schools. With regard to liberated mind, there is no distinction.

There are many different philosophical positions, and it's not necessarily the case that one is right and one is wrong. What is important is that a teaching further your understanding and benefit your mind. There are many ways of explaining reality at different levels of understanding.

Q. How can we use the description of the *skandhas* to look into our minds? Is it just a system of classification, or can we actually use it as a tool so that it will help us on the Vajrayana path?

A. There are many ways to use this teaching. The five *skandhas* are taught in a general sense to eliminate ignorance. The more you understand, the less ignorance you have. There are different meditative methods by which you can observe each of the *skandhas*. Kalu Rinpoche has also taught a special Vajrayana method of meditation on the five *skandhas*.

Q. Are the five *skandhas* related to the concept of mandala?

A. There is a very close relationship. The *skandhas* represent the impure aspects of things. When the *skandhas* are purified they manifest as a mandala, which is based on the five Buddhas and the five wisdoms. A famous teaching by Milarepa says that in its impure aspect, the world is the five *skandhas*; in its pure aspect, it's the five Buddhas; in its impure aspect, it's the five emotional afflictions; in its pure aspect, it's the five wisdoms.

Important to the Secret Mantra Vajrayana are the elements of symbol and meaning. Symbol is example—like mandalas and tanka [thang ka] paintings. Meaning is what is actually experienced in one's practice. The attainment of the stage of Buddhahood really has to do with one's own stream of being when it is purified, not when it is impure. Following the example of symbolic transformation, one brings about liberation through the meaning of one's practice.

Principally, the teaching of the five *skandhas* destroys ego-clinging, which is synonymous with the emotionally afflicted consciousness. All Dharma is taught as a remedy to ego-clinging. As attachment to the self becomes stronger and stronger, it becomes the main cause of our immeasurable suffering and unhappiness. On the other hand, you experience peace and happiness to the extent to which your clinging has lessened.

Tilopa* was not a man of many words. He would say very little to his student Naropa. But he did tell him that appearances are not the cause of our bondage to samsara. What binds us to samsara is our attachment to those things, and it is that which we must cut. Attachment to external sense impressions and an internal ego only binds one more and more to existence, and especially to the lower realms. To the degree that we can reduce our attachment, life improves: we are able to meditate and practice the Dharma more easily, and gradually extricate ourselves from the cycle of existence and suffering.

Kalu Rinpoche teaches that one should eat inferior food, wear tattered clothing, and so forth. In that way, one will be much happier and have less suffering. Rinpoche himself has no need for fine things, and whenever he sees his students with fancy clothes or possessions he is displeased. He doesn't say too much about this, but he really doesn't approve of vanity.

It is really true that if you want to be a good Dharma practicioner, you shouldn't have many activities and be very busy with all sorts of plans and things to remember all the time. When I was little, I was very happy because I didn't have anything to worry about; all I owned were some texts. I had no money, and just maintained a very simple practice of Dharma and meditation. Later on, I became

---

*The Indian Mahasiddha, teacher of Naropa. Naropa's quest for, and discipleship to, Tilopa are rich sources for stories about the difficulties that the Lama contrives in order to train his student.

busy and had much work to do, so I now know how difficult activity can be.

Meditation Practice

Let us complete our study with a short period of meditation on the shortcomings of samsara. This is an unhappy subject, so while you are meditating on this, you should sit in the position that I am in now, with one knee bent, elbow resting on knee, and head in hand—the posture of sorrow.

The six realms of samsara are completely filled with suffering, without even a hair's tip of happiness, like a pit of blazing fire. Wherever one might be reborn, there is only suffering. Reflect in detail on the sufferings of the each of the realms. For example, think of the fact that those in the god realm have to foresee their rebirth in the lower realm of suffering; that human beings suffer birth, illness, old age, and death; that animals are forced into service, or kill and eat each other; that hungry ghosts endure intense hunger and thirst; that hell-beings undergo unbelievable heat and cold. There is no enduring happiness whatsoever in any part of Samsara, whether it be the lower realms or even the higher realms.

Although suffering plagues all the realms, beings in the three lower realms are completely engulfed in it. There, through the cause of powerful hatred, desire and stupidity, suffering is unavoidable; it cannot be circumvented by any means. In our present lives we feel a great deal of pain if our skin is pierced by a needle or if we are out in the cold for a day; but those in the hells undergo kalpas of extreme heat and cold and excruciating pain.

If we go for a day or two without food and water, we know how difficult this is. But in the hungry ghost realm, beings have no control over their environment, and they have to go for unimaginable lengths of time without even a drop of water. We should reflect deeply upon such suffering.

As for animals, they are either constantly fighting with each other or hunting, killing and eating each other. Human beings force some of them to work; their state is one of perpetual fear and unhappiness.

In the human realm, even here in America, one of the best places a human being can be, there is suffering of all kinds. There are many luxuries which may give us some physical comfort, but mental happiness is really very hard to find, and there isn't a single person who doesn't have some kind of suffering or problem. Consider this, and then think of humans living right now in other countries and situations, people who are very poor, who don't have all the things that they need, and who have much more suffering. Finally, all humans, no matter what their situation, have sickness, old age and death.

In their realm, the Asuras continually fight with the gods; they are embroiled in jealousy and constantly suffer the pains of making war. The gods in the lower part of the sixth, highest, realm are those who fight the Asuras, and so they also suffer this combat. In the upper part of the gods' realm, there are tremendous luxuries and a feeling of happiness. Yet there is also latent suffering, because once the god's stock of merit has been exhausted, he must fall back into one of the other five realms of suffering. Thus, suffering is pervasive even in the higher realms.

Think about these various realms of samsara. Feeling fear at the prospect of being born in one or another of them, you begin to wonder, "How can I possibly get out of this cycle? What method can prevent me from experiencing this suffering?" Reflect that this is not your problem alone: all beings face this situation, including your mother and father and every other sentient being. Generate great compassion for their situation.

Now visualize that in the space in front of you, your own Root Lama appears in the form of Chenrezi. He says, "The nature of samsara is like a hot, burning fire. You need to bathe away the suffering of the lower realms by means of compassion." You then pray, "I have been wandering in samsara for a very long time. Now that I am practicing your teaching, with your great kindness please help me to enter the Buddha's Pure Realm." Promise that you will help all sentient beings to enter the Pure Realm also, and will not just save yourself.

Then imagine that light rays emanate from Chenrezi's heart, touch your heart, and guide you to the Pure Realm of Dewachen. Next, light rays come from your heart and touch all sentient beings in the universe, leading them to Dewachen. In this way meditate undistractedly on great compassion.

Now, sit in good meditation posture. From among the five *skandhas*, concentrate on the skandha of consciousness. Meditate undistractedly on mind's lucid awareness. Its essence is empty, its aspect is clear, and its nature is unimpeded.

Now that we have finished, we should dedicate the merit. When one meditates or explains the Dharma, it is important to share whatever roots of virtue one has accumulated with all living beings. In addition we should also make prayers of aspiration for the ultimate attainment of Buddhahood for everyone; for the world to be free of sickness, war, and famine; that the precious teaching of the Buddha endure and those who promulgate it live long.

OUTLINE OF THE FIVE SKANDHAS

I. FORM (zuk chi pung po [gzugs kyi phung po]) rupaskandha (Skt.)

    A. *Four Types of Causal Form* (ju yi zuk [rgyu'i gzugs])
        1. Earth (sa [sa])
        2. Water (chu [chu])
        3. Fire (me [me])
        4. Wind (lung [rlung])

    B. *Eleven Types of Resultant Form* (dray bu zuk ['bras bu'i gzugs]), divided into three main categories:
        1. The Five Sense Faculties (wang po nga [dbang po lnga])
        2. The Five Sense Objects (ton nga [don lnga])
        3. The Eleventh Form (zuk chu chik pa [gzugs bcu gcig pa])

        a) *The Five Sense Faculties*
            (1) Eye Faculty (mik ki wang po [mig gi dbang po])
            (2) Ear Faculty (na way wang po [rna ba'i dbang po])
            (3) Nose Faculty (na yi wang po [sna'i dbang po])
            (4) Tongue Faculty (che yi wang po [lce'i dbang po])
            (5) Body Faculty (lu chi wang po [lus kyi dbang po])

        b) *The Five Sense Objects*
            (1) Sights (zuk [gzugs])
                (a) Classified by color
                (b) Classified by shape
            (2) Sounds (dra [sgra])
                (a) Sentient sounds
                (b) Unsentient sounds
                (c) Venerable sounds
            (3) Smells (tri [dri])
            (4) Tastes (ro [ro])
                (a) Sweet
                (b) Sour
                (c) Bitter
                (d) Salty

      (e) Acid
      (f) Astringent
    (5) Tactiles (rek ja [reg bya])

  c) *Eleventh Form*
    Some examples of the Eleventh Form:
    (1) Atomic Form (dul tra rab chi zuk [rdul phra rab kyi gzugs])
    (2) Imagined Form (kun tak chi zuk [kun btags kyi gzugs])
    (3) Form Seen Through Meditation (wang jor way zuk [dbang 'byor ba'i gzugs])
    (4) Unapparent Form, e.g., the form of vows (rik che ma yin pay zuk [rig byed ma yin pa'i gzugs])

II. SENSATION (tsor way pung po [tshor ba'i phung po] vedanaskandha (Skt.)

  A. *Bodily Sensations* (lu chi tsor wa [lus kyi tshor ba])
    1. Pleasurable
    2. Painful
    3. Neutral

  B. *Mental Sensations* (yi chi tsor wa [yid kyi tshor ba])
    1. Pleasurable
    2. Painful

III. RECOGNITION (du she chi pung po ['du shes kyi phung po]) samjnaskandha (Skt.)

  A. *Two Aspects*:
    1. Identification (ton la tsen mar dzin pa [don la mtshan mar 'dzin pa])
    2. Differentiation (ta nyay la tsen mar dzin pa [tha snyad la mtshan mar 'dzin pa])

  B. *Three Scopes*
    1. Small (Objects within the Desire Realm) (chung ngu [chung ngu])

2. Extensive (Objects within all the Realms of Samsara) (ja che wa [rgya che ba])
3. Immeasurable (Only accessible to beings of the Formless Realm and beyond, i.e., Buddhas) (tsay me [mtshad med])

IV. FORMATION (du che chi pung po ['du byed kyi phung po]) samskaraskandha (Skt.)
These 51 states may be: virtuous, unvirtuous, neither, or variable.

A. *The Five Pervasive Mental States* (kun dro nga [kun 'gro lnga])
  1. Intention (sem pa [sems pa])
  2. Concentration (yi la che pa [yid la byed pa])
  3. Contact (rek pa [reg pa])
  4. Sensation (tsor wa [tshor ba])
  5. Recognition (du she ['du shes])

B. *The Five Determinative States* (yul nge che nga [yul nges byed lnga])
  6. Resolution (dun pa ['dun pa])
  7. Interest (mö pa [mos pa])
  8. Recollection (dren pa [dran pa])
  9. Samadhi (ting nge dzin [ting nge 'dzin])
  10. Wisdom (she rap [shes rab])

C. *The Eleven Virtuous Mental Occurrances*
  11. Faith (tay pa [dad pa])
    a) Faith of Yearning (dö pay tay pa ['dod pa'i dad pa])
    b) Trusting Faith (yi che pay tay pa [yid ches pa'i dad pa])
    c) Clear faith (dang way tay pa [dang ba'i dad pa])
  12. Carefulness (pa yö pa [bag yod pa])
  13. Thorough Training (shin tu jang wa [shin tu sbyang ba])
  14. Equanimity (tang nyom [btang snyoms])
  15. Sense of Propriety (ngo tsa she pa [ngo tsha shes pa])
  16. Considerateness (trel yö pa [khrel yod pa])
  17. Non-attachment (ma chak pa [ma chags pa])
  18. Lack of Hatred (she dang me pa [zhe sdang med pa])
  19. Lack of Stupidity (ti muk me pa [gti mug med pa])

20. Complete Harmlessness (nam par mi tse wa [rnam par mi 'tshe ba])
21. Diligence (tson dru [brtsön 'grus])

D. *The Twenty-Six Unvirtuous Mental Occurences*

The Six Root Defilements (tsa way nyön mong druk [rtsa ba'i nyon mongs drug])
22. Ignorance (ma rik pa [ma rig pa])
23. Desire (dö chak [dod chags])
    a. Desire of Desire (in Desire Realm) (dö pay dö chak ['dod pa'i 'dod chags])
    b. Desire for Existence (in Upper Realms) (si pay dö chak [srid pa'i 'dod chags])
24. Hatred (she dang [zhe sdang])
25. Pride (nga jal [nga rgyal])
26. Doubt (te tsom [the tshom])
27. View (ta wa [lta ba])
    a) View based on the perishable aggregates. i.e., a belief in a self (jig tsok la ta wa ['jig tshogs la lta ba])
    b) View of holding to extremes (eternalism or nihilism) (tar dzin pay ta wa [mthar 'dzin pa'i lta ba])
    c) Opposite view (lok par ta wa [log par lta ba])
    d) Holding one's own views as supreme (ta wa chok dzin [lta ba mchog 'dzin])
    e) Holding one's morality and discipline as supreme (tsul trim tang tul shuk chok dzin [tshul khrims dang brtul zhugs mchog 'dzin])
    Views are further distinguished as:
    (1) Innate (len chay [lhan skyes])
    (2) Acquired (kun tak [kun btags])

The Twenty Subsidiary Emotional Afflictions (nye way nyön mong nyi shu [nye ba'i nyon mongs nyi shu])
28. Wrath (tro wa [khro ba])
29. Malice (kon du dzin pa [khon du 'dzin pa])
30. Rage (tsik pa ['tshig pa])
31. Vindictiveness (nam par tse wa [rnam par 'tshe ba])
32. Jealousy (trak dok [phrag dog])

33. Deceitfulness (yo [gyo])
34. Hypocrisy (ju [sgyu])
35. Shamelessness (ngo tsa me pa [ngo tsha med pa])
36. Inconsiderateness (trel me pa [khrel med pa])
37. Concealment (chap pa ['chab pa])
38. Greed (ser na [ser sna])
39. Vanity (jak pa [rgyags pa])
40. Lack of faith (ma tay pa [ma dad pa])
41. Laziness (le lo [le lo])
42. Carelessness (pa me pa [bag med pa])
43. Forgetfulness (je ngay [brjed ngas])
44. Lack of conscience (shay shin min pa [shes bzhin min pa])
45. Fogginess (muk pa [rmugs pa])
46. Wildness (gö pa [rgod pa])
47. Distraction (nam par yeng wa [rnam par gyeng ba])

E. *The Four Variable Occurrences* (shen jur shi [gzhan gyur bzhi])
48. Sleep (nyi [gnyid])
49. Remorse (jö pa ['gyod pa])
50. Investigation (tok pa [rtog pa])
51. Examination (chö pa [dpyod pa])

V. CONSCIOUSNESS (nam she chi pung po [rnams shes kyi phung po] vijnanaskandha (Skt.)

A. The Eight Types:
1. Eye consciousness (mik ki nam she [mig gi rnam shes])
2. Nose consciousness (na yi nam she [sna'i rnam shes])
3. Ear consciousness (na way nam she [rna ba'i rnam shes])
4. Tongue consciousness (che yi nam she [lche'i rnam shes])
5. Body consciousness (lu chi nam she [lus kyi rnam shes])
6. Mind consciousness (yi chi nam she [yid kyi rnam shes])
7. Afflicted consciousness (nyön mong yi chi nam she [nyon mongs yid kyi rnam shes])
8. Basic consciousness (kun shi nam she [kun gzhi rnam shes])

Appendix 2

Glossary

It is important to note that the definitions in this glossary are intended to identify and clarify technical terms only as they are used in this book. They are in no way comprehensive definitions applying to all Buddhist usages. Many of the terms have significantly different senses in other contexts and other Buddhist traditions.

Direct quotations, unless otherwise noted, are drawn from the chapters of this book and are introduced here to serve as reminders of fuller discussions in the text.

Abhidharma (Skt.) chö ngön pa [chos mngon pa] (Tib.) The section of Buddhist scriptures concerned with philosophical, cosmological, and psychological analysis.

Ālayavijñāna *see* Kün shi nam she

Anuttarayogatantra (Skt.) nal jor la na me pay jü [rnal 'byor bla na med pa'i rgyud] (Tib.) "The highest of the four levels of Vajrayana teachings."

Arhat (Skt.) dra chom pa [dgra bcom pa] (Tib.) One who has "conquered the enemy," that is, the "emotions and ignorance that keep one locked in Samsara." The Arhat represents the Hinayana ideal, one who has experienced the cessation of suffering.

Asuras (Skt.) lha min [lha min] (Tib.) Envious gods who occupy a realm adjacent to the human realm in Samsara. "They live in continual strife," beset by possessiveness, paranoia, and jealousy of the gods.

Avalokiteśvara *see* **Chenrezi**

Bardo [bar do] (Tib.) Literally, "between two." In general, any interval, a "between." Six bardos are usually spoken of in the Vajrayana teachings:

1. The Death Process (Tib.: chi kay bar do ['chi kha'i bar do]) The interval from the moment when the individual begins to die until the moment "when the separation of the mind and body takes place."
2. The Chö nyi Bardo (Tib.: chö nyi bar do [chos nyid bar do])
   The interval of the ultimate nature of phenomena (the Dharmata), when the mind is plunged into its own nature. The first phase of the after-death experience.
3. The Bardo of Becoming (Tib.: si pay bar do [srid pa'i bar do])
   The interval in which the mind moves towards rebirth.
4. The Bardo between Birth and Death (Tib.: che shi bar do [skye shi'i bar do])
   Ordinary waking consciousness during the present lifetime.
5. Dream (Tib.: mi lam bar do [rmi lam bar do])
   The dream state we experience in sleep.
6. Meditative concentration (Tib.: sam ten bar do [bsam gtan bar do])
   The state of meditative stability.

Recently in the West "bardo" has been used to refer only to the first three of these, that is, the states between death and rebirth. These states are no more and no less illusory than dreams and ordinary waking consciousness.

Bhikṣu *see* **Gelong**

Bhūmi (Skt.) sa [sa] (Tib.)
Literally "ground." One of the ten stages of realization and activity through which a Bodhisattva progresses towards Enlightenment. The ten *bhūmis* are:

1. The Supremely Joyful (Tib.: rap tu ga wa [rab tu dga' ba]; Skt.: pramuditā).
2. The Stainless (Tib.: dri ma me pa [dri ma med pa]; Skt.: vimalā).
3. The Illuminating (Tib.: ö che pa ['od byed pa]; Skt.: prabhākarī).
4. The Radiant (Tib.: ö tro wa ['od 'phro ba]; Skt.: arcismatī).
5. Very Difficult to Train For (Tib.: shin tu jang ka wa [shin tu sbyang dka' ba]; Skt.: sudurjayā).
6. The Manifesting (Tib.: ngön du jur pa [mngon du gyur pa]; Skt.: abhimukhī).
7. The Far Going (Tib.: ring du song wa [ring du song ba]; Skt.: dūramgamā).
8. The Unwavering (Tib.: mi yo wa [mi gyo ba]: Skt.: acalā).
9. Excellent Intelligence (Tib.: lek pay lo drö [legs pa'i blo gros]; Skt.: sādhumatī).
10. Cloud of Dharma (Tib.: chö chi trin [chos kyi sprin]; Skt.: dharmamehga).

Bindu *see* Tig le

Bodhicitta (Skt.) chang chup chi sem [byang chub kyi sems] (Tib.)
The Enlightened Attitude proclaimed by the Mahayana — the *aspiration* to rescue all sentient beings from the sufferings of cyclic existence and bring them to Enlightenment, and *perseverance* in deeds and practice towards that end. The development of the Enlightened Attitude is an indispensable part of all Vajrayana practice as well.

Bodhisattva (Skt.) chang chup sem pa [byang chub sems dpa;] (Tib.) One who has taken the great vow to rescue all beings from suffering and guide them to Enlightenment.

Body of Completely Ripened Karma nam min ji lü [rnam smin gyi lus] (Tib.) The body of the individual regarded as a result of his own past acts, the "seemingly solid, concrete projection of mind that is the physical body."

Chem che [skye mched] (Tib.) āyatana (Skt.) field of sense perception. There are twelve fields: one for each of the six sense faculties, and one for each of their sensory objects.

Che nay bardo [skye gnas bar do] (Tib.) The bardo of the birth process. See *Bardo*.

Che rim [bskyed rim] (Tib.) utpattikrama (Skt.) The development phase of meditation, q.v.

Che shi Bardo [skye shi'i bar do] (Tib.) The bardo between birth and death. *See* Bardo.

Che wa [skye ba] (Tib.) Birth. The eleventh Nidāna, q.v.

Chenrezi [spyan ras gzigs] (Tib.) Avalokiteśvara (Skt.) The Bodhisattva of Compassion.

Chi ka Bardo ['chi kha'i bar do] (Tib.) the Bardo at the time of death. *See* Bardo.

Chin kor *see* Maṇḍala

Chö nyi Bardo [chos nyid bar do] (Tib.) *See* Bardo.

Clarity sal wa [gsal ba] (Tib.) One of the three intrinsic qualities of mind. the other two being Emptiness and Unimpededness; it corresponds to the Sambhogakāya (q.v.) aspect of Enlightenment, and is the mind's "inherent ability to experience."

Compassion nying je [snying rje] (Tib.) karuṇā (Skt.) Three levels of compassion are identified in the Mahayana:

1. Compassion with reference to all sentient beings.
2. Compassion with reference to all phenomena.
3. Completely non-referential or objectless compassion.

Daśabhūmi (Skt.) sa chu [sa bcu] (Tib.) The ten stages of Bodhisattva realization. (*See* Bhumi).

Dependent Origination ten drel [rten 'brel] (Tib.) praṭitya samutpāda (Skt.) A central insight of Buddhism, the interdependent co-origination of all things. (*See* nidana.)

Development State of Meditation che rim [bskyed rim] (Tib.) utpattikrama (Skt.) The development phase of Vajrayana meditation, in which a visualization of a deity is built up and maintained.

Dewachen [bde ba can] (Tib.) Sukhāvatī (Skt.) The Pure Realm of Amitabha Buddha.

De wa chen po [bde ba chen po] (Tib.) mahāsukha (Skt.) Supreme Bliss — the "direct experience of the nature of mind and its intrinsic purity."

Dharma (Skt.) chö [chos] (Tib.) Among the many meanings of *Dharma* in Sanskrit and *Chos* in Tibetan, three are especially important:

1. The whole body of the Buddha's teaching, usually capitalized in English.
2. Any constituent of a moment of existence, a "thing" or phenomenon.
3. Truth, or ultimate reality. (*See* Dharmakāya.)

Dharmadhātu (Skt.) chö ying [chos dbyings] (Tib.) The realm of all phenomena, the "dharma space" in which all transpires.

Dharmakāya (Skt.) chö chi ku [chos kyi sku] (Tib.) One of the Trikāya (three "bodies") of a Buddha: the body of Dharma. It "is equivalent to the ultimate" truth and is also expressed as the intrinsic emptiness of mind. Although it is without form and distinct from all activity (trö tral [*spros bral*]), it manifests the Sambhogakāya and Nirmāṇakāya to fulfill the aims of sentient beings.

Dharmatā (Skt.) chö nyi [chos nyid] (Tib.) The fundamental nature of all phenomena, all experience just as it is.

Dorje [rdo rje] (Tib.) vajra (Skt.) "Something invincible, something that can cut through anything else." Literal referents of vajra (a word cognate with English *vigor*) are "thunderbolt" and "diamond." The dorje or vajra is a Vajrayana ritual implement symbolizing method.

Dorje Chang [rdo rje 'chang] (Tib.) Vajradhāra (Skt.) The form in which the Buddha or the Lama manifests when giving Vajrayana teachings. Dorje Chang is the ultimate source of all the Buddhist tantric teachings.

Dorje Phagmo [rdo rje phag mo] (Tib.) Vajravārāhī (Skt.) The main Yidam of the Kagyu tradition, she is the embodiment of Wisdom.

Dorje Sempa [rdo rje sems dpa'] (Tib.) Vajrasattva (Skt.) "He whose being is of the nature of the Vajra," the Buddha of Purification. Vajrasattva Meditation, one of the Four Preliminary Practices, involves acknowledging all one's unskillful negative actions and attitudes, and aims to eradicate the habitual tendencies from which they arise.

Dra chom pa *see* Arhat

Drup khang [sgrub khang] (Tib.) "Practice building"—an enclosure used for intensive meditation and practice, particularly during the Three Year Retreat, q.v.

Du che ['du byed] (Tib.) saṁskāra (Skt.) The configuration of patterns in the mind which normally result in action (Karma) The fourth *skandha*, Formation.

Dzo rim [rdzogs rim] (Tib.) sampannakrama (Skt.) Fulfillment phase of meditation.

Eightfold Noble Path pak pay lam yen lak je ['phags pa'i lam yan lag brgyad] (Tib.) The eight aspects of the path of pure uncompromising behavior discovered in the Four Noble Truths.

1. Perfect View (Tib.: yang dak pay ta wa [yang dag pa'i lta ba])
2. Perfect Intention (Tib.: yang dak pay tok pa [yang dag pa'i rtog pa])
3. Perfect Speech (Tib.: yang dak pay ngak [yang dag pa'i ngag])
4. Perfect Activity (Tib.: yang dak pay lay chi ta [yang dag pa'i las kyi mtha'])
5. Perfect Livelihood (Tib.: yang dak pay tso wa [yang dag pa'i 'tsho ba])
6. Perfect Effort (Tib.: yang dak pay tsöl wa [yang dag pa'i rtsol ba])
7. Perfect Mindfulness (Tib.: yang dak pay dren pa [yang dag pa'i dran pa])
8. Perfect Samadhi (Tib.: yang dak pay ting nge dzin [yang dag pa'i ting nge 'dzin])

Emotional Affliction nyön mong pa [nyon mongs pa] (Tib.) kleśa (Skt.) Conflicting emotions which produce the misery and turmoil of existence. The emotions are usually given as three: desire-attachment (dö chak ['dod chags]), aversion (she dang [zhe sdang]), and bewilderment or indifference (ti muk [gti mug]).

Empowerment wang [dbang] (Tib.) abhiṣeka (Skt.) Ritual initiation into a particular practice of meditation, conferred by a Lama who is part of a lineage, and thus himself a recipient and practitioner of such transmissions. Authorization to engage in the meditative practice is not complete without the formal instruction and textual transmission (*see* tri and lung).

Emptiness tong pa nyi [stong pa nyid] (Tib.) śūnyatā (Skt.) The absence, in beings and objects, of independent existence and enduring self-nature; the essential quality of mind, corresponding to the Dharmakāya aspect of Enlightenment. Emptiness is the central theme of the Prajñāparamitā texts and Mādhyamaka philosophy, q.v.

Enlightenment chang chup [byang chub] (Tib.) bodhi (Skt.) Complete enlightenment is a state of Realization in which the most subtle traces of ignorance about the nature of reality are eliminated; sometimes called "the embodiment of the Three Kāyas," q.v. There are degrees or stages of Enlightenment; *see* Bhumi.

Five Certainties nge pa nga [nges pa lnga] (Tib.) Five attributes of the Sambhogakāya Buddha:

1. The form of the Teacher is eternal.
2. The environment is always a Pure Realm.
3. The teachings transmitted are always Mahāyāna or Vajrayāna.
4. The audience is always composed of beings on the eighth, ninth, or tenth Bodhisattva stages.
5. The manifestation is not subject to time; it is unchanging.

Five Families, Buddhas of the

Vajra Family	Akṣobhya (Skt.)	Mi-bskyod-pa (Tib.)
Lotus Family	Amitābha (Skt.)	'Od-dpag-med (Tib.)
Buddha Family	Vairocana (Skt.)	rNam-par sNang-mdzad (Tib.)
Jewel Family	Ratnasambhava (Skt.)	Rin-chen 'byung-gnas (Tib.)
Karma Family	Amoghasiddhi (Skt.)	Don-yod grub-pa (Tib.)

Five Paths, The *see* Paths, The Five

Form Phase of Meditation *see* Development Stage

Formless Phase of Meditation *see* Fulfillment Stage

Four Dharmas of Gampopa A "concise survey of the entire Path" to Enlightenment:

1   The Mind Turns Towards Dharma
2. The Dharma Becomes the Path
3. The Path Dispels Confusion
4. Confusion Arises as Primordial Awareness

Four (Ordinary) **Foundations** tün mong gi ngön dro shi [thun mong gi sngon 'gro bzhi (Tib.) *see* Four Thoughts that Turn the Mind

Four Names *see* ming shi pung po

Four Noble Truths pak pay den pa shi ['phags pa'i bden pa bzhi] (Tib.) Four fundamental insights of Buddhism, proclaimed in the Buddha's first teachings:

1. *Suffering* of conditioned existence.
2. Its *origin*.
3. Its *cessation*.
4. The *path* leading to cessation.

Four Thoughts that Turn the Mind [to the Dharma] lo do nam shi [blo ldog rnam bzhi] (Tib.) *see* Preliminaries

Fulfillment Stage of Meditation dzo rim [rdzogs rim] (Tib.) sampannakrama (Skt.) The completion or fulfillment phase in which the visualization is dissolved and the mind rests in the emptiness of its true nature.

Gampopa (1079–1153) [sgam-po-pa] (Tib.) Tibetan philosopher-saint. He initially trained as a physician (and hence is often called Dakpo Lharje [dvags po lha rje], "the Physician from Dakpo"). After the death of his wife he entered a monastery where he became a scholar in the Kadampa [bka' gdams pa] tradition of Atiśa. He later became a disciple of Milarepa, and a great meditator. He united the Kadampa teachings with the teachings of the Mahāmudrā tradition — "the uniting of the two streams (chu wo nyi dray [chu bo gnyis 'dres])." This union resulted in the Dakpo Kagyü [dvags po bka' brgyud] tradition, of which he was the founder. His *Jewel Ornament of Liberation* is an authoritative and complete account of the

Mahayana Buddhist path. Gampopa was the main teacher of the first Karmapa. Düsum Khyenpa.

Ga shi [rga shi] (Tib.) jarāmaraṇa (Skt.) Old age and death. The twelfth Nidāna, q.v.

Ge long [dge slong] (Tib.) bhikṣu (Skt.) A monk who has taken the full ordination. A similarly ordained nun is a gelongma [dge slong ma] or bhikṣuṇī.

Ge tsül, Ge tsül ma, *see* Novice

God lha [lha] (Tib.) deva (Skt.) Inhabitant of the least painful of the Six Realms of Samsara. The lives of gods, while long and marked by sensuous bliss, are ended in great sorrow as they foresee their future lower rebirth. There are gods of the Desire, Form and Formless Realms, q.v.

Gompa [sgom pa] (Tib.) Literally, "to meditate." Third phase of practice, which follows receipt of teachings and instruction (see *töpa)* and effort made to comprehend them (*see* sampa). *Gompa* is the actual pursuit of meditational practice.

Guru Yoga (Skt.) la may nal jor [bla ma'i rnal 'byor] (Tib.) One of the Four Preliminary Practices (see *Preliminaries*). A meditation in which through visualization and recitation the meditator receives the blessing of the Lama and the lineage.

Heart Sutra chom den day ma she rab chi pa rol tu chin pay nying po [bcom ldan 'das ma shes rab kyi pha rol tu phyin pa'i snying po (Tib.) Bhagavati Prajñāparamitāhṛdaya (Skt.) The extremely concise statement of the doctrine of Emptiness, regarded as the heart or essence of the vast Prajñāparamitā (Perfection of Wisdom) Literature. In many Mahayana traditions, the sutra is chanted regularly.

Hīnayāna (Skt.) tek pa chung wa [theg pa chung ba] (Tib.) One of the three "vehicles" of Buddhism—the "lesser" vehicle, or way of the

Arhat. In Tibetan usage, the name identifies an imperfect or incomplete quest for a purely personal liberation from samsara.

Human Birth *see* Precious Human Birth

Impermanence *see* Mi tak pa.

Interdependence of Phenomena *see* Dependent Origination

Instruction *see* Tri

Jamgön Kongtrul the Great (1813–1899) ['jam mgon kong sprul blo gros mtha' yas] (Tib.) Great Tibetan scholar and meditation master, an initiator of the *ri may* movement, *q.v.* Besides his many original texts and commentaries, he collected and edited an enormous wealth of rituals and practices and compiled the *Shay Ja Dzö* [shes bya mdzod], the great encyclopedia of Dharma, including history, art, lineages, and tantra, which is one of the *Five Great Treasuries* (dzö chen nam par nga [mdzod chen rnam par lnga]).

Jñāna *see* Yeshe

Kagyü [bka' brgyud] (Tib.) One of the major Tibetan schools, well represented in the contemporary Tibetan diaspora in Europe and North America. It has many sects and sub-sects — two such are the Dakpo Kagyü, founded by Gampopa, and the Shangba Kagyü, founded by Chungpo Naljor.

Kālacakra (Skt.) dü chi kor lo [dus kyi 'khor lo] (Tib.) Literally, "the Wheel of Time." A cycle of complex teachings embracing cosmology, history, psychology, and spiritual practice in one coherent system. Name of a tantra and of the deity featured in it.

Kalpa (Skt.) kal pa [bskal pa] (Tib.) A vast stretch of time.

Karma (Skt.) lay [las] (Tib.) Literally, "action." The sum of all an individual's deeds, which ineluctably determine their experiences during this life and in the afterlife and future births. Positive karma (merit) can be increased and negative karma eliminated through meditation and the practice of virtue, especially the six Paramitas.

Karma Chamay Rinpoche [ka rma chags med rin po che] (Tib.) A seventeenth century Tibetan teacher, disciple of the Sharmapa Chöchi Wangchuk, and author of a celebrated aspiration prayer and practice concerning Dewachen. He founded the Nemdo [gnas mdo] Kagyü sect, and was famous for Chenrezi and chö [gcod] practices.

Kāyas, Three ku sum [sku gsum] (Tib.) Trikāya (Skt.) "Three aspects of the totality of the completely enlightened experience." The three bodies or modes of existence of a Buddha. *See* Dharmakāya, Sambhogakāya, Nirmānakāya.

Khenpo [mkhan po] (Tib.) The chief instructor or spiritual authority in a monastery. Though the word is often translated as "abbot," the khenpo is not usually the administrator of the monastery. The title is also accorded to Lamas of great learning.

Kün shi nam she [kun gzhi'i rnam shes] (Tib.) Ālayavijñāna (Skt.) "Fundamental discursive consciousness," grounded in ignorance (ma rik pa [ma rig pa]). A repertory of habitual ways of thought, it "functions as a storehouse for the karmic process."

Kün shi ye she [kun gzhi ye shes] (Tib.) Primordial, panoramic awareness.

Lama [bla ma] (Tib.) guru (Skt.) A title for experienced and learned religious teachers, often casually used for members of the clergy in general. (Tibetans take the word as *la na me pa* [bla na med pa], "insurpassable," plus *ma* [ma], "mother," alluding to the compassion a mother has for her only child.)

Laypersons ge nyen [dge bsnyen] (male), ge nyen ma [dge bsnyen ma] (female) (Tib.) upāsaka (male), upāsikā (female) (Skt.) Buddhists who have taken the five basic vows of lay ordination, which abjure killing, stealing, lying, the use of intoxicants, and sexual misconduct.

Len pa [len pa] (Tib.) upādāna (Skt.) Grasping. The ninth Nidāna, q.v.

Lha tong [lhag mthong] (Tib.) vipaśyana (Skt.) Meditation that develops insight into the nature of mind. It is sometimes described as analytical meditation. It is one of the two types of meditation found in all Buddhist traditions, the other being tranquility meditation (śamatha, Skt.; shi nay [zhi gnas], Tib.; *q.v.*)

Lung [lung] (Tib.) Textual transmission. It is one of the three necessary components of Vajrayāna empowerment (*see* Empowerment and Tri). It is the (usually quite rapid) recitation aloud by a competent master of the text of the teaching or practice. It is intended to infuse the whole of the text, purely and accurately, into the mindstream of the hearer.

Liberation *see* Enlightenment

Mahāmudrā (Skt.) cha ja chen po [phyag rgya chen po] (Tib.) The "great symbol" or "great seal," a term in Vajrayana Buddhism for the realization of the true nature of mind. Mahāmudrā means both the ordered series of practices and meditations, and the awakened state of enlightenment to which they lead.

Mahāsiddhas (Skt.) drup chen [grub chen] (Tib.) Great Indian tantric masters renowned for effecting changes in the phenomenal world through spiritual power (see Dowman, trans., *Masters of Mahamudra*). They came from all walks of life and developed the means by which the Dharma could be effectively practiced by people of widely varying capacities and inclinations. Tilopa and Naropa are among the best known, and of central importance in the Kagyü tradition.

Maṇḍala (Skt.) chin kor [dkyil 'khor] (Tib.) A complex symbol that configures all the energies, aspects, and manifestations of a particular embodiment of enlightenment. The term also refers to two- or three-dimensional representations of such configurations, e.g., the Mandala of the Peaceful Deities.

Mantra (Skt.) ngak [sngags] (Tib.) Verbal expressions of enlightenment. Recitation of them aloud is understood as the "divine sound
or speech." "The speech of the deity is the embodiment of the union
of speech and emptiness."

Marikpa [ma rig pa] (Tib.) āvidyā (Skt.) Ignorance of the true
nature of mind. Fundamental ignorance, which leads to a belief in a
personal self.

Marpa Lotsawa (1012–1097) Marpa the Translator. Disciple of the
Mahāsiddha Naropa, Marpa was a Tibetan layman who made three
arduous trips to India to find Buddhist teachings. It was he who
brought the Six Yogas of Naropa to Tibet. Marpa received
Mahāmudrā transmissions from both Naropa and Maitripa, and
achieved highest realization. His chief disciple was Milarepa. (See
The Life of Marpa, Prajna, 1982.)

Middle View u ma [dbu ma] (Tib.) Mādhyamaka (Skt.) A
philosophical school based on the Prajñāpāramitā sutras and their
doctrine of emptiness [śūnyatā]. The Mādhyamaka is concerned
with the transcendence of affirmation and negation both, and
stresses the Dependent Origination of all things. The classic for-
mulation of the Middle View (between the extremes of assertion and
negation) is Nāgārjuna's *Mūlamādhyamakakārikās* (Root Verses on
the Middle Way).

Milarepa [mi la ras pa] (Tib.) Most famous of Tibetan yogis,
Milarepa was a layman, revered as one who achieved full enlightenment in one lifetime. He sang the songs compiled in the *Gur bum*
[mgur 'bum] (*The Hundred Thousand Songs*). Milarepa was the
disciple of Marpa the Translator, and was the teacher of Gampopa.
See *The Hundred Thousand songs of Milarepa,* G.C.C. Chang,
trans., and *The Life of Milarepa,* ed. and trans. by L. Lhalungpa.

Mi lam Bardo [rmi lam bar do] (Tib.) The Bardo of the Dream State. *See* Bardo.

Ming shi pung po [ming bzhi'i phung po] (Tib.) The *skandhas* of the four names. The first four stages in the Bardo of the After-death experience: ignorance, stirring of conscious patterning, discursive consciousness, and labelling subject and object (Skt.: āvidyā, saṁskāra, vijñāna, nāmarūpa).

Ming zuk [ming gzugs] (Tib.) nāmarūpa (Skt.) Name and form. The fourth Nidāna, q.v.

Mi tak pa [mi rtag pa] (Tib.) Impermanence. The impermanence of all conditioned existence is one of the basic Buddhist insights, and the teaching of impermanence characterizes all Buddhist traditions. In the present context, impermanence is one of the Four Thoughts that turn the mind towards the Dhrma.

Monk *see* Gelong

Nāgārjuna (Skt.) Lu drup [klu grub] (Tib.) Great Indian Buddhist scholar, logician, and philosopher who left Nalanda University to become a wandering yogi and eventually a Mahāsiddha. Known as the founder of the Mādhyamaka school and transmitter of the Prajñāparamitā literature on which it was based, Nāgārjuna is believed to have flourished during the second century A.D.

Nam she [rnam par shes pa] (Tib.) vijñāna (Skt.) Discursive consciousness: "the ability of the mind to recognize something other than itself as an object." This is our ordinary consciousness. The fifth *skandha*.

Naropa (1016–1100) Disciple of Tilopa and teacher of Marpa. A Bengali, he showed early promise as a scholar. He became a monk, and eventually Abbot of Nalanda, one of the great Indian Buddhist universities. After eight years he abandoned the academic life and became a wandering mendicant yogi, in search of his true teacher. After much difficulty, he encountered the Mahāsiddha Tilopa, from whom he learned the higher Tantras and Mahāmudrā.

Ngöndro [sngon 'gro] (Tib.) *see* Preliminaries

Nidāna (Skt.) The twelve nidānas are the "links of dependent origination that form the basis for a description of our experience of the world." They constitute the successive stages of dependent origination and are a central component of the Buddhist analysis of mind and experience. These are the twelve:

1. Ignorance (Tib.: ma rik pa [ma rig pa]; Skt.: āvidyā)
2. Formation of karmic habitual tendencies (Tib.: du che ['du byed]; Skt.: saṁskāra)
3. Dualistic consciousness (Tib.: nam she [rnam par shes pa]; Skt.: vijñāna)
4. A sense of embodiment (Tib.: ming zuk [ming zgugs]; Skt.: nāmarūpa)
5. Differentiation of sense-fields (Tib.: chem che [skye mched]; Skt.: sadāyatana)
6. Contact (Tib.: rek pa [reg pa]; Skt.: sparśa)
7. Sensation (Tib.: tsor wa [tshor ba]; Skt.: vedanā)
8. Craving (Tib.: se pa [sred pa]; Skt.: tṛṣṇā)
9. Grasping (Tib.: len pa [len pa]; Skt.: upādña)
10. Becoming (Tib.: si pa [srid pa]; Skt.: bhāva)
11. Birth (Tib.: che wa [skyed ba]; Skt.: jāti)
12. Aging and death (Tib.: ga shi [rga shi]; Skt.: jarāmaraṇa)

Nirmāṇakāya (Skt.) trül pay ku [sprul pa'i sku] (Tib.) third of the Trikāya or Three Bodies of a Buddha. A Buddha manifests in an infinite variety of forms in response to the individul needs of sentient beings. The three main classifications of Nirmāṇakāya are:

1. Manifestation as a skill, craft, or artistic talent;
2. Manifestation as an apparently ordinary being with a special capacity to help others (*see* Tülku);

3. Manifestation as a Buddha such as the historical Buddha Shakyamuni, born in the world and active therein.

In whatever form, the Nirmāṇakāya represents "mind's quality of unimpeded manifestation."

Nirvāna (Skt.) nya ngen lay day pa [mya ngan las 'das pa] (Tib.) Transcendence of suffering; cessation of birth in Samsara.

Norbu Döndrup [nor bu don 'grub] (Tib.) Kalu Rinpoche's Root Lama, retreat master of the Palpung Three Year Retreat. He was a disciple of Jamgön Kongtrul the Great and the lineage holder of the Shangba tradition. His life was devoted to meditation and retreat. At his death, in the early 1950s, he manifested the rainbow body.

Novice ge tsül [dge tshul] (male), ge tsül ma [dge tshul ma] (female) (Tib.,) śramaṇera (male), śramaṇerikā (female) (Skt.) One who has taken monastic ordination, but without the full range of vows. Usually, a novice will eventually take full monastic ordination.

Nyingmapa [rnying ma pa] (Tib.) One of the four main traditions of Tibetan Buddhism. For Nyingmapas, Padmasambhava (Guru Rinpoche or precious Lama) is the central figure in whom they take refuge. The name of their school ("older ones") reflects their adherence to the earliest translations of Buddhist texts into Tibetan.

Obscuration drip pa [sgrib pa] (Tib.) vāraṇa (Skt.) What is obscured is the true nature of mind. Four levels of obscuration are spoken of in this text:

1. Obscuration of Fundamental Ignorance ma rik pay drip pa [ma rig pa'i sgbrib pa] (Tib.) āvidyāvāraṇa (Skt.) "The mind does not see itself, it is not directly aware of its own nature."
2. Obscuration of Habitual Tendencies bak chak chi drip pa [bag chags kyi sgrib pa] (Tib.) vāsanāvāraṇa (Skt.) Based on ignorance, mind develops "the habit of experiencing reality in terms of subject and object."
3. Obscuration of Emotional Affliction nyön mong pay drip pa [nyon mongs pa'i sgrib pa] (Tib.) kleśavāraṇa

(Skt.) Confronted by these dualistic projections, mind reacts with attachment, aversion and bewilderment.

4. Obscuration of Karma lay chi drip pa [las kyi sgrib pa] (Tib.) karmavāraṇa (Skt.) Emotional confusion produces physical, verbal, and mental reactions that become habitual and have their own further consequences.

Palpung [dpal spungs] (Tib.) A major monastic center in Kham, residence of the Situ incarnation lamas. The retreat center started there by Jamgön Kongtrul was presided over later by Kalu Rinpoche.

Paths, The Five

1. Path of Accumulation tso lam [tshogs lam] (Tib.) sambhāramārga (Skt.) The first phase of effort towards enlightenment: purifying one's obscurations, acquiring merit, and achieving emotional and meditative stability—"gathering what we need for the journey."

2. Path of Application jor lam [sbyor lam] (Tib.) prayogamārga (Skt.) Practice of twenty-two of the thirty-seven elements of enlightenment, *q.v.*

3. Path of Vision tong lam [mthong lam] (Tib.) darśanamārga (Skt.) The first level of Bodhisattva realization. "Instead of seeing things in the ordinary sense, one actually sees the nature of mind."

4. Path of Meditation gom lam [sgom lam] (Tib.) bhāvanāmārga (Skt.) This path, with the preceding, coincides with the ten stages of Bodhisattva realization.

5. Path of No More Learning mi lop pay lam [mi slob pa'i lam] (Tib.) aśaikṣamārga (Skt.) Buddhahood.

Peace shi wa [zhi ba] (Tib.) śānti (Skt.) A synonym for Nirvāṇa.

Perfection of Wisdom *see* Prajñāparamitā

Prajñāparamitā The "Perfection of Wisdom," a name for the body of Mahayana sutras expounding the doctrine of Emptiness; among the most famous of these are the *Heart Sutra* and the *Diamond Sutra*. Also, the name of the female Buddha (she rap pa rol tu chin ma [she rab pha rol tu phyin ma]) who represents perfect wisdom.

Pratimokṣa (Skt.) so sor tar pa [so sor thar pa] (Tib.) Originally, the rules and directions for conscientious moral conduct by which the members of the Sangha are to live. In the present context, the word suggests (as the Tibetan says literally) "the discipline of *individual liberation.*"

Precious Human Birth Human birth that possesses the Eight Freedoms and Ten opportunities. The Eight Freedoms are freedom from birth in any of the eight unrestful states; that is, not to be born:

1. As a hell-being
2. As a *yidak*
3. As an animal
4. As a god
5. In a society where the Dharma is unknown
6. As a person with wrong views, who believes in neither Dharma nor karma
7. In an age when no Buddha has appeared
8. As a person suffering from mental or sensory impairments that make it impossible to understand the Dharma

Of the Ten Opportunities, or Resources, five refer to one's personal condition and five to one's environment. One is born:

1. As a human
2. In a country where the Dharma exists
3. With one's senses and intelligence intact
4. Without karmic compulsions to commit evil deeds
5. As a person able to have faith in the Three Jewels
6. In an age in which a Buddha has appeared
7. In an age in which a Buddha has taught the Dharma
8. In an age in which the Dharma has not declined, but endures
9. In a region where many practice the Dharma

10. In a region where others, motivated by faith and kindness, will help one in one's practice

The Precious Human Birth is extremely rare; while hell-beings, for instance, are said to be as numerous as atoms, *yidaks* as the sands of the Ganges, animals as snowflakes, and gods of the higher realms as stars in the night sky, those having the Precious Human Birth are said to be as rare as daytime stars.

Preliminaries The Ordinary Preliminaries for Mahāmudrā are meditations on the Four Thoughts that Turn the Mind (to the Dharma). These are:

1. The Precious Human Birth (*q.v.*) with its freedoms and opportunities.
2. Impermanence and the inevitability of death.
3. The pervasiveness of suffering (*q.v.*) in saṁsāra.
4. The inerrancy of karma.

The four Extraordinary Preliminaries are:

1. Taking Refuge and making prostrations to the Three Jewels and the Three Roots, *q.v.*
2. Dorje Sempa purification, *q.v.*
3. Maṇḍala Offering, *q.v.*
4. Guru Yoga, *q.v.*

The Ordinary and Extraordinary Preliminaries are together termed *Ngöndro* [sngon 'gro] in Tibetan.

Preta *see* Yidak

Primordial Awareness *see* Yeshe

Protectors chö chong [chos skyong] (Tib.) Embodiments of wisdom, usually represented as wrathful or terrifying in appearance, who are invoked to eliminate obstacles on the path to Enlightenment. They are among the wisdom beings, third of the Three Roots in Vajrayāna refuge. The most important protector for the Kagyü tradition is Mahākāla.

Pure Land dak pay shing kam [dag pa'i zhing khams] (Tib.) The sphere of activity of a Buddha. A Buddha-Realm where sentient beings mature towards enlightenment.

Raptu Gawa [rab tu dga' ba] (Tib.) pramuditā (Skt.) "Total joy:" the first stage [*bhūmi*, q.v.] of Bodhisattva realization.

Realization *see* Enlightenment

Realms of Saṁsāra, the Three kam sum [khams gsum] (Tib.) tridhātu (Skt.)

1.	Desire Realm:	Extends from the lowest hells up to certain of the gods' realms.
2.	Form Realm:	The seventeen levels of the gods of form.
3.	Formless Realm:	Four levels of the formless gods.

Refuge chap [skyabs] (Tib.) śaraṇa (Skt.) To take Refuge (chap su dro wa [skyabs su 'gro ba]) is to make a formal commitment to accept the precepts and protection of the Three Jewels as the way of developing the aspiration for enlightenment. In the Vajrayana, one also takes refuge in the Three Roots.

Renouncing and Accepting pang lang [spangs blang] (Tib.) Giving up unvirtuous actions and adopting the course of virtuous conduct.

Rek pa [reg pa] (Tib.) sparśa (Skt.) Contact, or touch. The sixth Nidāna, *q.v.*

Ri may [ris med] (Tib.) A syncretic movement in nineteenth century Tibet intended to minimize sectarian rivalry and revitalize spiritual practice by making use of texts, commentaries, and procedures from many different Tibetan traditions. Jamgön Kongtrul, Chokchur Lingpa, Mipham Rinpoche, and Khyentse Wangpo are among the best known of the ri may masters.

Rinpoche [rin po che] (Tib.) Literally, "precious" one. A title reserved properly for incarnate lamas (*see* Tülku) and eminent spiritual teachers. It is used both as a term of address and as the last element in the name.

Ro chik [ro gcig] (Tib.) ekarasa (Skt.) *Ro chik* is the third of the four phases of Path Mahāmudrā: One Point, Free from Activity, One Taste, and No More Meditation.

Root Lama tsa way la ma [rtsa ba'i bla ma] (Tib.) A teacher from whom one has received the empowerments, instructions, and precepts that form the core of one's own practice.

Sakya [sa skya] (Tib.) One of the four major sects of Tibetan Buddhism. Its most famous teacher was Sakya Pandita. The lineage stresses intellectual preparation and meditation.

Samādhi (Skt.) ting nge dzin [ting nge 'dzin] (Tib.) Meditative concentration.

Śamatha *see* Shi nay

Sambhogakāya (Skt.) long chö dzok pay ku [long spyod rdzogs pa'i sku] (Tib.) The illuminating potential of mind. Second of the Three Bodies of a Buddha, it is emanated from the Dharmakaya to benefit sentient beings on the path by providing an example of the goal. The Sambhogakāya manifests only to Bodhisattvas. *See* the Five Certainties.

Samdrup Tarjay Ling [bsam 'grup dar rgyas gling] (Tib.) Kalu Rinpoche's monastery in Sonada, a hill town near Darjeeling in West Bengal.

Sam pa [bsam pa] (Tib.) Literally, "to think about." Second phase of practice: contemplating what has been taught, and applying it thoughtfully and alertly to one's experience.

Saṁsāra (Skt.) kor wa ['khor ba] (Tib.) Cyclic existence, the beginningless and endless wheel of rebirth.

Sam ten Bardo [bsam gtan bar do] (Tib.) The Bardo of meditative stability, equilibrium. *See* Bardo.

Sangdok Palri [zangs mdog dpal ri] (Tib.) The Noble Copper-Colored Mountain, the Pure Land of Guru Rinpoche.

Sangye [sangs rgyas] (Tib.) The Tibetan word for Buddha. It combines the notions of complete *purification* (*sangs*) and *rgyas, expansion* (that is, of knowledge).

Sangha (Skt.) gen dün [dge 'dun] (Tib.) The "assembly of practitioners who realize and transmit the [Buddha's] teachings." (sometimes a distinction is made: the whole body of the Buddhist clergy and Buddhist practitioners is the Sangha, while the Arhats and Bodhisattvas are the *Aryasangha*, the Noble or Exalted Assembly.)

Seed Syllable tsik [tshig] (Tib.) bīja (Skt.) A single syllable conceived of as the expression of one embodiment of enlightened mind; thus HRĪḤ is the seed syllable connected with Buddha Amitābha and the Bodhisattva Avalokiteśvara.

Sems [sems] (Tib.) citta (Skt.) One of several Tibetan words for mind. More specifically, it can denote the ālayavijñāna or Eighth Consciousness.

Sending and Taking tong len [gtong len] (Tib.) A method for developing bodhicitta. A meditation in which practitioners willingly take on all the pains and burdens of other beings, and willingly give out all that is positive in their own lives, their merit and happiness. The practice was promulgated in Tibet by Atiśa.

Se pa [sred pa] (Tib.) tṛṣṇā (Skt.) Craving. The eighth Nidāna, q.v.

Shangba [shangs pa] (Tib.) A lineage of Tibetan Buddhism, founded by the scholar-siddha (kay drup [mkhas grub]) Chungpo Naljor in the eleventh century. It emphasizes meditational practice and teaches the Five Golden Dharmas (Ser chö nga [gser chos lnga]), which include the Six Yogas of Niguma (comparable to the Six Yogas of Naropa, q.v.). The Shangba lineage has been important as a source of teachings and practice, rather than as an organized hierarchy or monastic sect, and its influence has been felt by all the traditional schools of Tibetan Buddhism. Kalu Rinpoche is the present lineage holder of the Shangba teachings.

Shangba Rinchen Dün Jü [shangs pa rin chen bdun rgyud] (Tib.) The "precious lineage of seven" who established and transmitted the Shangba teachings of Mahāmudrā.

1. Vajradhāra (Dorje Chang [rDo rje' Chang])
2. Niguma [Ni gu ma]
3. Chungpo Naljor [Khyung po rNal 'byor]
4. Mokchokpa [rMog lCog pa]
5. Chergangpa [sKyer sGang pa]
6. Nyentönpa [gNyan sTon pa]
7. Sangye Tönpa [Sangs rgyas sTon pa]

Shavari (Skt.) Sha wa ri pa [sha ba ri pa] (Tib.) One of the Indian Mahāsiddhas, said to have been a hunter reformed and instructed directly by Chenrezi. Achieving full realization after twelve years of meditation, Shavari chose to remain in this world for the benefit of all beings, and will remain until the next Buddha comes.

Shen pa Shi drel [zhen pa bzhi 'bral] (Tib.) "Separation from the Four Attachments," a teaching in the form of a simple quatrain, used in the Sakya tradition.

Si pa [srid pa] (Tib.) bhāva (Skt.) Becoming. The tenth Nidāna, q.v.

Six Yogas of Naropa Usual name for the Six Dharmas of Naropa (Naro Chödruk [na ro chos drug]), the yogic practices which constitute a basic part of the Kagyü traditions of training. The six, followed by their Tibetan names, are:

1. Psychic heat (tum mo [gtum mo])
2. The Illusory body (jü lü [sgyu lus])
3. Dream (mi lam [rmi lam])
4. Clear Light (ö sal ['od gsal])
5. Intermediate States (bar do [bar do])
6. Consciousness Transference (po wa ['pho ba])

Shi nay [zhi gnas] (Tib.) śamatha (Skt.) Tranquility meditation, which develops calmness of mind. One of the two basic meditations in all traditions of Buddhism, the other being vipaśyana (lha tong, q.v.).

Si pa Bardo [srid pa bar do] (Tib.) The intermediate stage of Becoming. *See* Bardo.

Six Realms The six planes of rebirth within Saṁsāra:

1. Hells
2. Realm of the Hungry Ghosts (*yidaks*)
3. Animal Realm
4. Human Realm
5. Realm of the Asuras
6. Realm of the Gods

The last three are called Fortunate Realms, while the first three are called Unfortunate.

Skandhas, The Five pung po nga [phung po lnga] (Tib.) Five aggregates that describe the physical and mental existence of all beings in the Desire Realm:

1. Form (Tib.: zuk [gzugs]; Skt.: rūpa)
2. Sensation (Tib: tsor wa [tshor ba]; Skt.: vedanā)
3. Recognition (Tib.: du shay ['du shes]; Skt.: saṁjñā)
4. Formation (Tib.: du che ['du byed]; Skt.: saṁskāra)
5. Consciousness (Tib.: nam shay [rnam shes]; Skt.: vijñāna)

Skandhas of the Four Labels *see* Ming shi pung po.

Songtsen Gampo (ca. 569–650) [srong btsan sgam po] (Tib.) King of Tibet. Tibetan historians considered him an emanation of Chenrezi and a powerful monarch of Asia.

Suffering du ngal [sdug bsngal] (Tib.) duḥkha (Skt.) Three types of suffering are described:

1. The all-pervasive fundamental suffering: "the suffering of simply being alive." (chap pa du je chi du ngal [rkyab pa 'du byed kyi sdug bsngal])
2. The suffering of change (jur way du ngal ['gyur wa'i sdug bsngal]).
3. The suffering of suffering, i.e., actual pain (du ngal chi du ngal [sdug bsngal kyi sdug bsngal].

Śūnyatā *see* Emptiness

Sūtra (Skt.) do [mdo] (Tib.) A scripture attributed to the Buddha Shakyamuni.

Tantras (Skt.) jü [rgyud] (Tib.) The root scriptures of Vajrayana Buddhism. The texts are ascribed to the Buddha Shakyamuni in various of his manifestations, and each usually describes the mandala and practice associated with a particular enlightened being. The word "tantra" literally means "thread" or "continuity."

Tārā Drölma [sgrol ma] (Tib.) A female Bodhisattva of Compassion, specially associated with the ability to protect her devotees and rescue them from suffering, fears, and dangers.

Targay Gyamtso Rinpoche [dar rgyas rgya mtsho] (Tib.) First Root Lama of Lama Norlha. Native of the small kingdom of Nang Chen in Kham. He spent sixty years in meditation and retreat, mostly in seclusion or in the mountains. He was a disciple of Jamgön Kongtrul, who called him "the Milarepa of Go Chi," referring to the monastery with which Targay Gyamtso was connected. He assumed the rainbow body in February 1959.

Tathāgata (Skt.) de shin shek pa [de bzhin gshegs pa] (Tib.) The "Thus-gone" one, an epithet for a Buddha.

Tathāgatagarbha (Skt.) de shin shek pay nying po [de bzhin gshegs pa'i nying po] (Tib.) The seed of Enlightenment, the potential for Buddhahood in every sentient being.

Tertön [gter ston] (Tib.) A discoverer of hidden texts (ter ma [gter ma]) understood to have been concealed by great teachers of the past in various ways, until the time when they could be understood and applied.

Thirty-seven Limbs of Enlightenment:
> Four essential recollections.
> Four proper attitudes towards what should be renounced and
> > what accepted.
> Four bases of supernormal power.
> Five strengths.
> Five faculties.
> Seven subsidiary factors.
> Eightfold Noble Path.

Three Jewels kön chok sum [dkon mchog gsum] (Tib.) Triratna (Skt.)

1. The Buddha, embodiment of Enlightenment.
2. The Dharma, the Buddha's teaching.
3. The Sangha, the Community of those committed to the practice of these teachings. This includes the ordinary human Sangha and the Noble Sangha of Bodhisattvas.

Three Roots tsa wa sum [rtsa ba gsum] (Tib.) In the Vajrayana, refuge is taken in the Three Roots: the Lamas, the Yidams, and the Protectors.

Three Year Retreat lo sum cho sum [lo gsum phyogs gsum] (Tib.) A fundamental discipline of training and spiritual practice. For three years, three months, and three days, retreatants devote themselves in seclusion to meditational practice and study.

Tig le [thig le] (Tib.) Bindu (Skt.) Literally, a "drop" or "circle," the word has a very wide range of referents. In this text, two usages are to be noted:

1. The circles or dots of light that appear to the mind in certain stages of the Bardo experience.
2. The red and white tig le, as the creative energy of the body, whose control and direction during yogic practice can result in the attainment of stable bliss.

Tilopa (988–1069) Indian Mahāsiddha, teacher of Naropa. Tilopa is considered the person in whom the lineage of Mahāmudrā became manifest. He received the teachings directly from Dorje Chang.

Tong len *see* Sending and Taking

Tö pa [thos pa] (Tib.) Literally, "to hear." First of the three phases of practice consisting of hearing (and reading and studying) the teachings.

Tri ['khrid] (Tib.) Instruction in the proper performance of a Vajrayana practice. *See* Empowerment.

Trungpa Rinpoche A line of incarnation Lamas long associated with Surmang [zur mang] Monastery in eastern Tibet. The present tülku, the eleventh, Chogyam Trungpa Rinpoche, lives and teaches in the West.

Tsor wa [tshor ba] (Tib.) vedanā (Skt.) Sensation or feeling, the feeling-tone of an experience. The seventh Nidāna, q.v.

Tsurpu [mtshur phu] (Tib.) A great monastery near Lhasa which was the seat of the Gyalwa Karmapas and headquarters of the Karma Kagyü linage. This function has been fulfilled in recent years by Rumtek monastery in Sikkim.

Tuk say [thugs sras] (Tib.) Heart-son; a close disciple or successor of a high Lama.

Tülku [sprul sku] (Tib.) One of the three types of Nirmāṇakāya. It usually denotes a being of high realization who deliberately chooses to be reborn in a specific situation for the benefit of sentient beings. The Dalai Lama and the Gyalwa Karmapa are well known examples.

Unimpededness man ga pa [ma 'gag pa] (Tib.) One of the three intrinsic qualities of mind, the other two being Emptiness and Clarity; the manifestation of the inseparable union of mind's essential Emptiness and natural Clarity; it corresponds to the Nirmāṇakāya aspect of Enlightenment. "The intelligence that allows us to make judgments and recognize particular details is a manifestation of mind's Unimpededness."

Union of Form and Emptiness One specific referent of this important notion is the meditational experience of the "apparent but in no way substantial form" of an image of Enlightenment, the Bodhisattva Avalokiteśvara, for example.

Vajra *see* Dorje

Vajradhāra *see* Dorje Chang

Vajrasattva *see* Dorje Sempa

Vajravārāhī *see* Dorje Phagmo

Vajrayāna dorje tek pa [rdo rje'i theg pa] (Tib.) the third of the Three Vehicles of Buddhism. Also called Mantrayāna, it is the Buddhism of Tibet, Mongolia, and much of the Far East, in which the central Mahāyāna themes of compassion and emptiness are dealt with using symbolic and practical systems of technique and understanding.

Vinaya (Skt.) dul wa ['dul ba] (Tib.) Buddhist scriptures concerned with monastic discipline and moral conduct; the code of virtuous behavior so presented.

Vipaśyana *see* Lha tong

Wang *see* Empowerment

Yama (Skt.) Shin je [gshin rje] (Tib.) The Lord of Death and judge of the afterlife, usually called Yamaraja (Shin je gyal po [gshin rje rgyal po]).

Yeshe [ye shes] (Tib.) jñāna (Skt.) Primodial awareness.

Yeshe Tsogyal [ye shes mtsho rgyal] (Tib.) Disciple and consort of Guru Rinpoche, and his Dharma successor.

Yi [yid] (Tib.) One of several Tibetan words for "mind." Here it designates the "impassioned or afflicted consciousness," which is the Seventh Consciousness when eight are reckoned.

Yidak [yi dvags] (Tib.) preta (Skt.) Hungry Ghosts, occupants of one of the three unfortunate realms of samsara (i.e., Hells, Hungry Ghosts, and Animals). The yidaks are tormented by unappeasable appetites.

Yidam [yi dam] (Tib.) Meditational deities who are embodiments of particular aspects of Enlightenment.

Index